SHOAL
BAY

GW00597751

ROBERTSON
BARRACKS

HOWARD
SPRINGS
→

STUART HIGHWAY

PALMERSTON

Darwin

Other titles in this series

Darwin

TESS LEA

NEWSOUTH

A NewSouth book

Published by
NewSouth Publishing
University of New South Wales Press Ltd
University of New South Wales
Sydney NSW 2052
AUSTRALIA
newsouthpublishing.com

National Library of Australia Cataloguing-in-Publication entry
Author: Lea, Tess, author.
Title: Darwin/Tess Lea.
ISBN: 9781742233864 (hardback)
       9781742241739 (ePub)
       9781742246772 (ePDF)
Subjects: Sociology, Urban – Northern Territory – Darwin.
          City and town life – Northern Territory – Darwin.
          Darwin (N.T.) – History.
          Darwin (N.T.) – Climate.
          Darwin (N.T.) – Social life and customs.
Dewey Number: 994.295

Design Josephine Pajor-Markus
Cover design Sandy Cull, gogoGingko
Cover image Lightning at Mindil Beach, William Nguyen-Phuoc
Image on pp.vi–vii Detail of 'Fragment' by Katrina Tyler, sculpture at the
       entrance to Darwin Convention Centre
Endpaper map David Atkinson, handmademaps.com
Printer Everbest, China

Contents

Preface

Darwin is a survivor, you have to give it that. Razed to the ground four times in its short history, it has picked itself up out of the debris to not only rebuild, but grow.

This book is my attempt to capture what this vulnerable, resilient city is about. It describes the marvellous contradictions of a place that is bloated by delusions of grandeur one moment and shrunken by needful humility the next. Darwin has known catastrophes and resurrections; it has endured misconceived projects and birthed visionaries. This is not going to be a tourist guide configured as a map of visitable sites, nor is it history told in strict chronological order. To know Darwin, to know its soul, you have to listen to it, soak in it, taste it. My account is inextricably tied to my own family history living and growing up in Darwin. It begins with the howl of Cyclone Tracy in 1974 and ends with the howl of fighter jets

— the destruction that was visited upon Darwin and the destruction Darwin threatens to visit upon others. These two howls map out the city in another way: archaic wildness at one end, future-tense technology at the other, poly-ethnic populations, exotic wildlife and political machinations in between.

There are many omissions. There are events that brought Darwin to international attention that I neglect. The place is infamous for the murders along its back roads, such as at Barrow Creek in 2001, when Peter Falconio was killed and his girlfriend Joanne Lees abducted, the young tourists bewitched by the sweet curves of a seemingly broken-down kombi van, a violent murderer tucked inside. Initially, Territorians had looked at Joanne with suspicion: did she display sufficient distress to be believable? We do that to outsiders. Take the time when a woman called Lindy Chamberlain was jailed in Darwin for allegedly killing her baby. She was released only after prolonged agitation about the dodgy forensic science and the guilt of dingoes. In the 1950s, Evdokia Petrov, wife of a KGB-agent-turned-spy, was spirited off her Russia-bound plane in Darwin, making our tarmac one of the defining images of the Menzies era. And let's not forget, the Beatles first touched down in Australia at Darwin airport too.

My feeling, rightly or wrongly, is that these events are less about Darwin the place and more about Darwin as a coincidental venue.

With minor exceptions, I also pay less attention to the town's political identities and celebrity characters. While some are artists, this isn't the place to offer a full account of Darwin's extraordinary creative scene either. That would take another book. Darwin's uniqueness has struck artists of all types with the need to express its distinction. The bombastic Xavier Herbert captured the town's early 20th century character and challenged Australians to think on their racial misdeeds. The reclusive painter Ian Fairweather, one of Australia's leading abstract artists, made the back end of a World War II supply ship beached at Frances Bay in Darwin his home for over a year, before setting out for Timor in April 1952 on a small raft made, like a Duchamp art object, from discarded refuse. Today, Trevor the Rubbish Warrior roams the streets of Darwin threading palm fronds and roadside rubbish into sculptural forms, as his temporary odes to homelessness. Suzanne Spunner lived in Darwin for over a decade and wrote a play,

Dragged Screaming to Paradise, about hating the place then loving it. There's the humorous, piercing critiques by artists Therese Ritchie, Todd Williams and Chips Mackinolty, drawing attention to the underside of Darwin's huntin', fishin', shootin' 'n' drinkin' character. And the extraordinary weavings of Aly de Groot as she takes ghost nets from the sea and asks us to think anew about the steaming waters that surround Darwin, and what humankind is brewing there. This list would explode as a starburst with Indigenous filmmakers, musicians, sculptors, dancers, actors and authors — a vibrant creativity which deserves its own focus. The truth is, I could find no sensible or fair way to select a symbolic few to write about, and anything attempting comprehension in such an abridged space just seemed vacuous.

The people whose stories I chose to highlight capture Darwin's uniqueness in different ways. They are not necessarily well-known identities but they have shaped the town even so. This ode to Darwin, my home town, is for locals and strangers alike. It shows the Darwin people know, one that might be unfamiliar, and aspects some don't want to know about. Darwin's insistent social disadvantage, so much a part of the city's past and present, comes in and out of view, for while Darwinites like to imagine theirs as an equal kind of place, it is born of inequalities too. Then again, if the city was more orderly, it would be far less tantalising.

Each chapter takes a theme – disasters and reinvention, real and imagined dangers, how the place is lived, and where it might be going – and weaves in accounts of the mixed forces that have shaped people and place. These 'mixed forces' – historical, geological, political, economic, human, non-human, local and global – are in play all at once and all the time. Even so, it is impossible to keep such abundant coexistences in simultaneous view or to give them equal billing. So while I do not believe humans operate on their own in shaping cities and have found place for some of Darwin's many critters, the book remains (misleadingly) people-centric.

In writing it, I accessed oral histories, spoke to new- and old-timers and, as an anthropologist who cannot understand worlds other than through participation, I took part in much of what I describe. I now work at the University of Sydney, commuting home as often as I can. In order to remind myself of Darwin's sensory forcefield, I sat in storms, sweated in the build-up and joined the arty types during the Dry Season's magnificent Darwin Festival. To give a sense of how Darwin was lived in earlier times, I studied footage in official archives and in published and private collections, and I kept on speaking to people.

I wrote as collaboratively as possible, wanting my words to warrant the trust of the storytellers, but in the end, this is a book about Darwin as I know it and responsibility for its views rests with me.

Building from the ruins

Bad Santa

The roof took seconds to peel upward, hurling metal and nails into the wild night. The external wall was next to go, opening my little-girl bedroom to a dark vortex, a world where missile ribbons of corrugated iron, trees, wires, shards of wood, car doors and lampposts were lashed to crazed dance by the spearing wind.

A small piece of wall cladding cracked, smashing down onto my splayed hands as I cowered on the bed. I clung to that cladding against the wild forces that would steal it back into the howl beyond. It was all that I had left for a ceiling, a futile shield against the screeching winds and black objects swirling in that wild night sky.

'MUM! DAD!' my sister and I cried, just as they swooped in, herding us downstairs to the relative safety of the kitchen, where I got to take my first sips of Tia Maria from the adults' celebration stock.

The screeching went on and on, for just over six hours, petering to a stop only after dawn.

It is this, the uncanny howl of shredding worlds, which most people remember about Cyclone Tracy. It was a sound of a thousand nails on chalkboards, the warning wail of the banshees, a keening and thrashing that foretold deaths and devastation. Before the anemometer instrument was itself destroyed, just after the eye of the cyclone passed through, the wind gauge at Darwin Airport officially recorded winds of 217 kilometres per hour.

Today, visitors can enter a cyclone room at the Northern Territory Museum and Art Gallery to take in a piece of that sound. Behind a corrugated iron screen tagged with faux post-cyclone graffiti, the museum visitor can listen to the disjointed sounds of a recording made by priest Ted Collins.

As he bunkered for the night at St Mary's Cathedral, Father Collins predicted the scraping of roof metal and roaring winds would be his end. I will make this recording, he thought, and perhaps they can find it in the morning.

It was a strange day, the day after the cyclone. Christmas Day 1974. The air was grey and heavy with moisture, the sun bleak. A desultory wind flapped at scraps of material; shredded plants sagged anew in the sodden air. Broken wires dangled from twisted electricity poles. At first people wandered about in a daze, dressed as they'd spent the night, the men in shorts, singlets or no shirts at all; the women braless, in nighties and cotton dresses. Others were still in their party clothes. Some were already picking through the piles of shrapnel for the salvageable.

Being a bush surveyor, my father had a Nissan Patrol, good axes, industrial wire-cutters and crowbars ready to hand. He set off to check on his parents and brother in Sabine Road, Nightcliff, carefully avoiding the debris littering Bagot Road, driving past the torn remnants of homes, past light aircraft draped over fences, past uprooted trees and corrugated iron sculptural ruins. My grandparents and uncle were still alive, the back half of their house blown apart.

Meantime, from our house in Brown Street, off Ross Smith Avenue in the now upmarket suburb of Parap, we could see all the way to the shell of what would be the new Darwin Hospital, miles away in the suburb of Tiwi. There were no visual obstructions. There was no fence around the Fannie Bay racecourse, no entry gates, no bush, no buildings. Just a flattened horizon strewn with wreckage, as if the town had once again been bombed. Even the green ants had disappeared.

The night's furious levelling revealed just how flat Darwin really is. Built on a small peninsula, the airfield occupies the highest and most desirable ground. Deeply weathered cliffs shield skinny bands of suburbs from the surrounding mudflats and swamps, an expanding delta which has been carving at the cliffs and extending further out to sea since the last ice age. These mangroves and waterways give Darwin its love/hate allure: the famous barramundi and waterbirds, the infamous crocodiles and the loathed mosquitoes, sandflies and midges.

Today, amid the dense rebuilding, another way to see Darwin's low relief is from the air. Approaching Darwin by plane, one can look down on the tortuous course of its waterways, twisting first this way, then that, lurching from side to side for want of a change in the level. With no gradient drops to force a straighter exit, the rivers, streams and creeks carve figures of eight as they wend their way out to sea, writhing like giant serpents.

The flat-lying sediments on which Darwin is perched are underlaid by ancient Proterozoic rocks that form part of the Australian 'craton' – the continental mass. The extended shelf keeps the seawater milky as equatorial tides drag over it, back and forth, before the edge of Australia drops into ink-dark ocean deeps just shy of Timor.

It is this original ancient land which forced molten magma up through flat surfaces to create the rich assortment of minerals which, together with militarisation, today sustains northern settlement. It is this intractable geography and climate that so knocks white settlers about. And it is this geology that makes Darwin the living paradox of being hot and swampy, yet arid for most of the year.

It is far less verdant than people imagine, with

only a few dwindling rainforest patches to match the western desire for a tropical aesthetic of palms, flowering trees, vines and cascading streams, and no mountains to attract year-round rain. The water-thirsty palms, green lawns and vivid flowers tourists marvel at are the product of modern reticulation systems and imported plants. The cultivated tropical veneer rubs off at the edges of the city, where it is replaced by spindly trees stunted by their battles with termites, sparse pandanus and organically depleted rust-red laterite soil, leached each year by the extremes of wet and dry.

During the Dry, leaf litter cracks underfoot into little shards against the unyielding baked ground, while grasses spear their seeds into the softer parts of foot flesh. During the Wet, Darwin's iron-rich soils invite one of the highest lightning strike rates in the world and roads become impassable, while the hot sea boils up the winds for the inevitable, devastating cyclones.

Both Father Collins and his sound recording made it through that night. While only 6000 of the 47 000 residents still had homes, the official death toll was small (though people still harbour suspicions of an undercount). Tracy came in on a low tide, so there was no surge to drown low-lying suburbs and, being a sodden Christmas Eve, with the rain already pelting down by six in the evening, most residents were tucked inside, celebrating or sleeping, before the cyclone hit.

Officially, only seventy-one people died. Yet many people left Darwin after that long night, traumatised to their core, never to return.

Les Liddell had been serving as a Unit Officer with the Tennant Creek Emergency Service when he heard news of Darwin's devastation. As the little town of 3000 people prepared for the unknown influx of refugees bound to head down the Stuart Highway, they had no idea of how many would come, or in what condition. The first man to drive in was still in his pyjamas. He had not dared to stop in Katherine: at 316 kilometres south of Darwin it was still too close to the terror he was fleeing. The man was still in shock. As Liddell later told the Northern Territory Archive Service, 'He said to me, he was looking out his kitchen window at two small children, a boy and a girl, and the boy was holding onto his sister's hair to try and stop her from blowing away when a sheet of iron came and cut both his arms off. He said, "And that was it."'

As Liddell tells it, the town of Tennant Creek

battled its own shortages and the exhaustion of volunteers working round the clock, yet little miracles counteracted the grim encounters. The people of Alice Springs were working hard too, raising money for the folk in Tennant Creek so the residents could manage the expense of running a first port of call, as hundreds came in, with no clothes or food, no spare tyres, no fuel. The Commonwealth, advised by Defence, had agreed to meet evacuation expenses, picking up the tab from Mount Isa to the east and Alice to the south. Since the folk at Tennant had orchestrated an emergency response without seeking official approval first, they were told the bills they were racking up would be theirs to pay. Without the public support of folk in Alice Springs, places like Tennant and the even smaller towns along the Stuart Highway would have been stripped bare. A modern-day version of a bucket brigade slotted into place.

Toward the end of the long fortnight's operation, Liddell took a phone call from the airport. It was three in the morning, the dark hour of catastrophic news. A plane was coming in to land with a peculiar request: could the pilot please have a pint of milk and a bucket of water? Liddell asked: 'Well, how many passengers have you got?' The pilot radioed back: 'Oh, don't you worry about the passengers; you just bring out the pint of milk and the bucket of water!'

The milk was for the pilot, the water for his passengers. Inside the Connellan DC-3 plane, down one side, sitting quietly with name labels and destination tags, was a row of dogs, tied up; cats huddled down the other side. Having survived Tracy with their owners, the animals were to be euthanised by official order. For many locals, this was yet another assault. The unknown pilot saved these lucky few. Says Liddell: 'They flew these animals from Darwin to Alice Springs, and then on to Sydney. And it was the greatest thing – a humane thing – I've ever seen, to see all these animals sitting quietly there in this aircraft.'

My family stayed safe; my cat, too. Huddled in our kitchen through that long, wild night, I sat on my brother's lap and our cat slept on mine, three tiers of mutual support. Snowball had rendered herself unconscious early in the night, waking only when it was all over. Other animals were not so lucky. Wounded stock had to be shot; pets had disappeared into the night. Police were ordered to shoot dogs on sight, as many had been let loose by fleeing inhabitants, or were assumed to be strays, whether they were or not. Dead marine animals swept in by the stormy waters and crushed against rocks started to rot on the beaches. The stench, like the sound, refuses writing. The odour comes to the tongue but not into words. But survivors recall the smell of rotting things, dead flesh rotting in wet ground, food putrefying without electricity, sodden materials rotting, sewer pipes dribbling and everywhere the dank clotting of mildew as vividly as they recall the terrifying howl of the wind.

As the cyclone gathered offshore, I was training in the Olympic pool across the road from our house. The pool manager had begun his Christmas revelries as we swimmers drilled up and down the familiar black line, bubbles swashing with each out-breath. Instead of threatening the naughty kids running on cement and dive-bombing unwary swimmers with rubbish duty or expulsion, that day the manager slurred cheerfully, raising his bottle to the microphone: 'Virsh a shyklone comin' tonight!' Next day, the pool was filled with the broken parts of Darwin.

The pool manager's relaxed attitude was typical. A warning about the impending cyclone had come through earlier that week and again that day. A cyclone named Selma (they were all given female identities back then) had come through three weeks earlier, but it was a fizzer, heading east without causing any damage. Cyclone Tracy warnings were duly broadcast but mostly ignored.

Given the authorities had so little impact, could we locals have known better? We all remember the stillness of the day before. The silence. How the birds had disappeared. But there were good reasons for ignoring all the signs.

Importantly, Darwin is a place where the imported seasonal markers of summer, autumn, winter and spring have no meaning. Locally, people note two main seasons: 'the Wet', a brief but intense monsoonal deluge from January through to March; and 'the Dry', a long drought extending from April through to September. By December, people are willing storms to break the searing heat and rising humidity that precedes the Wet. Locals call this bridge period 'the build-up', a reference both to the climbing humidity and temperatures, and the mounting stress of the sticky, sapping heat. Alternative names are mango madness, the silly season, even the suicide season.

It is as if the body registers as a psychic assault the lowering air pressure from thunderstorms brewing over warm water. The early 1970s were days without air-conditioning in schools, shops or houses; of vinyl seats in cars and no reticulation to make lawns plush. Adults drank beer and didn't bother with much clothing, for even cotton stuck to hot skin. Children ate frozen oranges and dived in and out of the local waterholes and backyard pools. Flooded drains would draw out whole neighbourhoods, kids bouncing into the shooting water as fearlessly as ducks, racing little sticks down the drains. We targeted sprinkler tripods on ovals, slicing the hot air with their interrupted sprays: szsh-szsh-szssssh. Storm drains, a broken drainpipe, a roadside fire hydrant. Kids swarmed over anything that banished the swelter.

You are in a stifling sauna, not a romance novel of languid afternoons under the palms. Your brain seems to be melting and tempers flare; irritability spreads from itching skin to the whole world. Only the fish, mozzies, fleas and cattle ticks are happy, breeding faster in the steaming heat.

But in the early Wet, a good storm pushes down a welcome rush of cold air. Raindrops soothe the broiling concrete paths and the tar on the roads stops melting. A heady smell of dust-mixed steam sends a message: the suicide season is over. Exuberant with the thrill of mating, frogs croak long into the night while gentle breezes flow over damp clothing, cooling and calming nerves brought to wit's end by the build-up of explosive heat. The early rains in December 1974 relaxed people: the build-up was broken, the monsoon had arrived. Time, at last, to celebrate.

Of course, it was also hard to get fussed about another cyclone, so soon after the false alarm of Selma and so very close to Christmas. The experience of strong storms appearing in the stead of cyclones had become so commonplace that plaintive engineers could not budge Canberra planners from declaring that Darwin was outside any cyclone zone. It took another cyclone to hit Townsville, also on a Christmas Eve, before tropical building codes contained any requirements for wind-proofing. Besides, Tracy was expected to do more or less the same as Selma: hit the town with some squally weather and then head on out to sea.

For a while that seemed to be Tracy's itinerary – that is, until the morning of 24 December, when the cyclone turned west rather than east and set a direct course for Darwin. By early Christmas Day, Darwin had ceased to function as a city. Two weeks later, following an official program of evacuation supervised by the military, less than one quarter of the population, 10 638 people, mostly men, were allowed to remain. Women and children were evacuated, whether they wanted to go or not.

My mother, older sister and I went on a plane to an army barracks in Brisbane on 30 December 1974. We were stabbed with needles immediately on disembarking, fears of cholera and typhoid galvanising nurses who handed out styrofoam cups brimming with barley sugar lollies as solace. We could take our pick from trestle tables laden with donated clothing. I chose a red velvet dress with long sleeves and white cuffs, and a pale blue satin shirt – materials the like of which I'd not seen (nor had any use for) in Darwin – and enjoyed the generous serves of jelly and ice-cream in the mess hall.

Meantime, Darwin had become a city without children. As local politician Dawn Lawrie put it, we 'realised then just what a dreadful act the Pied Piper had perpetrated on Hamelin'. Later, the

Commonwealth Department of Social Security commissioned psychological tests on survivors. It reported that those who had been evacuated suffered more than those who were allowed to stay and protect their homes and recover the odd belonging. Those who were evacuated and never returned suffered most of all: alone, unconsoled and with little hope of closure.

Survivors visiting the museum are rightly warned that listening to the priest's tape in the cyclone room might be distressing. For some, it rekindles their very worst memories. It does not affect me that way, but I took a friend in to see the exhibit, as part of her first return to Darwin, some three decades after the cyclone. Her mare, Princess, had been stabled at East Point Reserve, a cliff-top precinct famous for its sunset viewings, military history, its strip of vine forest, wild wallabies and up-market restaurant 'Peewees on the Point'. (A beer-drinking group of journalists used to settle with their eskies on an exposed piece of rock in the water off East Point and, as the sun set, down as much beer as their bodies could hold.

Their name? The Darwin Rocksitters Club.)

Princess had her rump sliced off by a piece of flying corrugated iron and had to be put down. For my friend, the cyclone room recalled her pony's excruciating end: how frightened poor Princess must have been, all alone and exposed to the night's missile-filled fury. Long after we left the exhibit, we groped through the silences and hacked words of her renewed grief. For others, the cyclone chamber is so removed from the full sensory experience of living through Cyclone Tracy, so banal, it should be removed altogether. One survivor, Cathryn, tells me: 'You need at least to have the walls shuddering, water running down them, drop the temperature by ten degrees, treble the volume and have things bashing into it. I would get rid of that display. It just makes newcomers complacent. I've heard people coming out of it saying, "Is that all?"'

Like the experience of Darwin itself, the cyclone is a personalised mode of knowing, which nonetheless unites everyone around a shared marker. Darwin's self-identity still pivots around pre- or post-cyclone reference points.

Today, you can gauge how seriously people are taking a cyclone warning by how intensely they shop. The supermarket shelves will be stripped bare of bottled water, batteries, matches, bandages and tins of baked beans. Servos will have their fuel sucked dry. Office workers are told to move important papers away from windows, clean up, secure all loose equipment and unplug their computers from the walls. At home, people create cyclone kits, tape their glass windows and batten down furniture. They toss their outdoor furniture into pools and create waterproof satchels in which to store precious possessions and important documents.

But what Darwin teaches you is profoundly simple. In the end, the beings you love, and how you remember them, is all that anyone needs to hang onto.

Australia's Pearl Harbor

Uniquely in Australian settlement history, Darwin has been destroyed four times: three times by air spinning in the same direction as the earth, forming deadly tropical cyclones, and once by Japanese bombs. Cyclone Tracy howled through one long night. The bombing of Darwin lasted nearly two long years, beginning in the morning of 19 February 1942. The Japanese dropped more bombs and sank more ships in Darwin's port than in Pearl Harbor, hit a mere three months before by the same commander and with the same squadrons.

It is one of the mysteries of Australian war history that the 'only significant battlefield of a modern mechanised war on Australian soil' is still in the process of being uncovered. The Australian population knew little about the attacks on its country. At first, southern readers were told fifteen people had been killed, twenty-four injured; that there were ninety-three planes in use, and only two raids. The raids, claimed the media, must have been launched from Papua New Guinea. There was no way the Japanese had the capacity to wage an aerial war from the sea. That they were the first in the world to coordinate aircraft from so many different sites into one hammer blow could not be admitted in White Australia.

Australia's most beloved war time Prime Minister, John Curtin, maintained the ruse:

> a severe blow has been struck in this first battle
> on Australian soil. It will be a source of pride
> to the public to know that the armed forces and

civilians conducted themselves with the gallantry that was traditional in people of British stock. We must face with fortitude the first onslaught and remember that whatever the future holds in store for us we are Australians and will fight grimly and victoriously ... Darwin has been bombed, but it has not been conquered.

Two weeks after the first air raids, the Lowe Royal Commission, appointed on 3 March 1942, provided more detail. The Commission estimated approximately 240 people were killed, and almost twice as many wounded, with the Japanese using 188 carrier-borne aircraft and fifty-four land-based bombers from Ambon. They also investigated, among other things, accounts of how many Australian Defence Force members abandoned their posts, looted the hospital and raided stores as they escaped. This is history almost covered up.

Given the role of Pearl Harbor in galvanising America's greater commitment to warfare, why the secrecy on our local attack? The answer has to do with Australia's unshakable faith in the mother country.

For centuries, sea power had enabled Great Britain to play an outsized role in international geopolitics. And even though the once great colonial predator was already heading toward redundancy, in Australian eyes British naval supremacy reigned. Darwin's oil and water tanks were installed in the 1920s precisely to help provision a British naval port in Singapore, enabling the Royal Navy to fend off any regional threat. This was Australia's 'Blue Water Strategy'. The faith outweighed the material investment. The oil tanks at Darwin's Stokes Hill sat unprotected and vulnerable from the time of their installation, suffering the indecision of a national government that knew it had to protect its fuelling base, yet was incapable of allocating the money. In the end, old cannons from disarmed ships were placed at East Point, to deter enemy vessels approaching the harbour from the sea. A raid from the air was unthinkable.

Playing down the bombing of Darwin and keeping silent about the full extent of the attacks was essentially a propaganda exercise to avert panic. During the war, at British government insistence, the most experienced Australian soldiers were fighting elsewhere. The country was already feeling vulnerable when Singapore, the key node in Australia's defence, was taken by the Japanese. Like Darwin's shore battery, the ammunition for the guns defending Singapore was meant for piercing ships. The fixation on naval approaches enabled the Japanese to arrive overland, swiftly take Singapore and imprison 15000 Australians – all less than a week before Darwin was bombed. Who could admit to such vulnerability after such prolonged faith in the illusory protections of Empire?

As with Cyclone Tracy, early warnings about the bombings also went unheeded. Aboriginal and missionary spotters from Bathurst Island and beyond radioed warnings about the Japanese aircraft flying overhead well before any alarm was sounded in Darwin. The Darwin sirens came only seconds before the first enemy attack in the history of British occupation of the Australian continent. It was 9.58 am on Thursday 19 February 1942. The belated sirens could not prevent the carnage. Just as survivors were emerging to inspect the damage, at midday, a second attack came.

There were only 2000 civilians living in Darwin at the time, for most of the women and children had already been evacuated. Yet while it was still only a fledgling military outpost, that morning the port was particularly congested. A convoy of ships carrying Australian and American troops and supplies had aborted an attempt to get to embattled Timor, fleeing an attack by Japanese aircraft and submarines. In a single morning, twenty military aircraft were shattered, eight ships at anchor in the harbour were sunk, and most civil and military facilities in Darwin were destroyed. Half the casualties were American, their bodies forever lost in saltwater graves.

Photos show billowing clouds of black smoke behind the wharf, belching plumes from direct hits to the tanks and all that leaking oil. The photographers remain anonymous but their viewpoint is almost always from the sea, the rare footage bequeathed by those with the obsessional nerve to focus a camera when hell is raining down.

There is a battle amongst historians about what happened next. There were dead bodies in the mangroves, out at sea and on the land. There were people crazed with fear, their town turned to rubble. Refugees fled by every means possible, leaving on foot, by bicycle, by vehicle, even stealing horses from stables as they tried to get away. Defence personnel also ran from the terror raining down from above and from what they were not trained for, these men who had made roads, dug drains, notated Morse code and fixed machinery but lacked experience operating weapons. Looters crashed through the glass panes of the shops that were still standing and smashed into hotel cellars, making off with what they could.

There was such disarray, the Australian government urgently appointed Justice Charles John Lowe of the Victorian Supreme Court to inquire into the raid, the extent of the damage and what needed to be done in the future. Over five intense days Commissioner Lowe examined seventy witnesses in Darwin, speaking later in Melbourne to an additional thirty. He discounted the rumours already in circulation that civilians, including the union members from the wharf, had mobbed a train in their cowardly rush to escape, saying if anything was to blame, it was lack of leadership. The police, the military and Administrator Aubrey Abbott had not been pulling in a united direction.

On Tuesday 19 February 2013, to mark the commemoration of the bombing of Darwin, I ignored the organised events at Darwin's purpose-built war cenotaph on the strip of land known as the

Esplanade and went across the harbour to the Aboriginal community of Belyuen, near the former government compound known as Delissaville. It took less than fifteen minutes to get across the water, but it had been a long time between visits. The last time I came by ferry I was a teenager, on a slower, bigger vessel. It had been a rough journey that time; the waves were running high. As the boat smashed against its moorings a passenger had her arm crushed between the ferry and a wooden pylon on the old Mandorah jetty.

On the 2013 anniversary of the bombing of Darwin, the water is calm and glassy, clear enough to see ballooning jellyfish wafting lazily through the water, their snowy grace belying their lethality. Few others were heading to Mandorah with me. The hotel on the other side is closed. Tourists don't visit at this time of year and there is no swimming during the long humid months of October through May.

It seemed fitting to share this commemorative day with Rex Sing, Linda Yarrowin, Trevor Bianamu and Robyn Lane, to hear their stories of Darwin, Delissaville and the war. They don't visit Darwin much these days, country they used to know as part of their nomadic estate, saying it has become too hostile for Aboriginal people, but they certainly know about the Japanese bombings. We sit on upturned milk crates under an African mahogany, speaking over the noise of chainsaws as a large tree that has grown too close to Rex and Linda's home is hewn. While the mahogany's shade is welcome, its shallow root ball and habit of dropping limbs are not. Linda begins: 'This is a true story, what mum told us, what they have been through, during that war. Our mob knew the bombing planes were coming across. They were really scared.'

Across the bay from Darwin, all the way from Delissaville, people could hear the sounds and see the black smoke billowing into the daytime sky, and knew it was no natural thing. Shortly after, they were forced onto trucks and trains and interned at war camps near Adelaide River and at Donkey Camp in Katherine.

'Were they happy to go?' I ask. I know that Delissaville was already an internment of sorts, where families up and down the coast had been forced into the one spot, to be trained as labourers and domestics. They had to labour in the garden, pulling weeds, digging holes, hand-watering from a well, to grow the cassava, snake beans, pineapples and bananas the settlement supervisors were always thrashing Aborigines to magic into existence from the unforgiving soil. They would hand-carry produce from the barge to the kitchens, up and down the rocky track, no matter how small or tired the carrying arms.

'Not really, they were made to, you know,' Rex says. 'They wanted to go back to *their* country, get away from Delissaville and from that bombing too.'

Linda agrees, returning to the story of her mother Ruby.

She did not want to come back to the Delissaville settlement, she didn't want to stay at Katherine in a war camp. She wanted to go back to her *own* country. So she walked back, with her parents, 300 kilometres, climbing up hills, to the coast, back to their own place at Daly River. Just to get away.

My mum was scared of all the white people, army and all that. They stole food to eat. Cabbages. She seen a lot of dead of bodies. Dead bodies were all over the place. And bombs were still happening. That's when they got really scared.

Linda's mum Ruby was only young as she made the long journey back, with her parents, all the way from Katherine, through Tipperary Downs and on to Anson Bay and the Cox Peninsula, avoiding the Stuart Highway, a different kind of Rabbit Proof Fence. They didn't like the way they had been treated in the camps or at the settlement and were homesick for the saltwater.

They had to make a canoe from wood and bark to cross the Daly River. 'It was windy, rough and dangerous, but they still made it.'

For Ruby Yarrowin, all non-Aboriginal people were suspect, not just Japanese pilots. Given how the most intimate aspects of Aboriginal life were habitually interfered with, there were threats far closer to home. Aboriginal women interned in war camps were preyed upon by servicemen demanding what men in the frontier always seemed to think was owing to them. The men had grabbing hands. The station owners could shoot at you. The settlement managers looked hungrily at your children, maybe figuring on taking them away. So as recently as 1972, when Linda was born at Darwin Hospital, the same place as I was, her mother Ruby saw no point in staying. The nurses and doctors were part of the same system that sent Aboriginal people to work camps in the name of re-education and protection. Ruby fled the uniformed staff and closed walls, certain they represented potential harm. While Linda survived the lack of clinical neonatal care, she tells me some of her siblings did not.

I was trying to find out where my grandfather fitted into all this, by interviewing my father, Billy Lea, about Pop. Bill is an old man now, but his blood is still stirred by memories of the Territory. He took his maths brain into the outback, where love of numbers became love of cattle, beer and horses and reckoning the lie of the land, staring at the sun through a theodolite and measuring by the stars. I knew Pop had something to do with the navy and the fuel storage tanks down at Stokes Hill Wharf, where the Darwin peninsula begins, and where the bombings were targeted. Dad's stories came out in jumbled order, telling a tale of chance, danger and drinking – a typical Top End narrative.

His father, incongruously named Henry Joseph Lea (otherwise known as Tocker) joined the navy in the 1920s after serving in the army during World War I. He had endured the Depression by escaping out to sea. One month before the bombing of Darwin, he was on HMAS *Wollongong*, a navy escort corvette. It was the last Australian ship to leave Singapore, escaping by the narrowest of margins — half an hour, according to Bill. Corvettes were crowded, all-purpose ships, designed for anti-submarine warfare, minesweeping, escort, freight and other do-as-you're-told roles. On the race back to Fremantle, a tanker they were escorting ran aground on a reef west of Tanjung Priok, Batavia. HMAS *Wollongong* stayed behind in the doleful hope of towing the stranded tanker off at high tide. They tried and failed over and over to haul the tanker off the reef, until their efforts were unceremoniously terminated by Japanese air attack. Carnage ensued. The ships that had gone ahead were all obliterated. Survivors from one burning death ship were rescued by another that was annihilated the next day.

'Just remember,' Bill tells me at another point, 'just remember in the navy when they went into the action phase the seamen were bolted in. No wonder the old coot drank.' He chuckles as he tells me this, yet this heavy drinking is part of the Darwin story too. Men self-medicating in the hard-living frontier, where psychic scarring is accepted and does not have to be confessed.

Darwin was a place where pasts were not probed into, the 'capital of the second chance'.

War trauma was something I never thought about, visiting my grandparents in their house on Sabine Road. When did the sweaty, puffy-faced old man known to me as 'Pop' get his naval tattoos? What would he have told me if I'd interrupted the beer drinking and asked questions over that loud radio, relentlessly tuned to the horse races and the cricket? How many other Darwin men wore their battle scars in the truculent oblivion of drink?

By 1946, as a non-commissioned seaman at the age of fifty, my Dad's old man had become too old to stay in the navy. A mate on the Naval Board offered him familiar all-purpose work as a foreman restoring the fuel tanks at Darwin's port, working not for the navy but as a civilian. The prospect of better pay, no uniform and no need to salute clinched the deal. So, like the discharged navy men who had filled the posts as Darwin's early Resident Administrators, Tocker took the job — only he was no uptown governor but a working-class man who could down a slab of beer a day. He bade his wife join him from Sydney, four young children in tow: two boys, two girls. Another son would soon be born in Darwin. It was

August 1946 and civilian life had barely started.

Seven of the eleven fuel oil storage tanks were destroyed by the Japanese air raiders. In the belated rush to provide an alternative to the exposed tanks during the war, expensive and ultimately ineffective underground storage tunnels had also been excavated. Immediately corroding and admitting water, they were never put into use.

Today, tunnels five and six are marketed as an exciting opportunity for self-guided tours. They can be reached via Darwin's new waterfront precinct, part of an ongoing government quest to build tourism as a viable economic contributor. Despite the tunnels' role in my origins, I avoided them until five years ago. Feeling like a stranger in my home town, one day I headed for the umbrella shade structure on Kitchener Drive, where a man steeped in humid lethargy sold entry tickets and handed out a limp, disposable brochure.

Inside, the tunnels retain their original signs and labels. The dank walls have thick pipes joined with large bolts. Here and there are little doors and ladders and photos of the air strikes; but the most dominating sensation is of musty stale air, miserable light and rust-coloured puddles.

The storage tanks were defeated by the

unforgiving claims of the northern climate. The salted air that eats metal, the torrential water that cracks rocks, leaving dripping cement tunnels no good for keeping fuel. It is a harsh instruction on materiality – another lesson Darwin insistently teaches its residents. Don't bring valuable things to this place: they will get eaten.

Pop was needed to tend the newly repaired out-door fuel tanks. All except one had an unexploded bomb underneath.

'Sounds like pretty dangerous work, mucking around with fuel tanks and unexploded bombs?' I suggest.

'Hmm,' Bill murmurs, noncommittally. Then casually adds, 'I know there was a bomb nearest to our house, about 40 to 50 metres away. And how we never got mixed up with that stuff – asbestos – because everything was covered with asbestos powder, I'll never know.'

My grandmother's greatest concern was to find the bullets first. She would prise them from the walls of their house at Stokes Hill Wharf before her brat boys found them, a favourite game being to smash live ammo between rocks or explode them in fires. The house was honeycombed with bullet holes and missing bits of wall. The boys pushed their beds around to find the driest spots from incoming rain and went into battle with the mosquitoes and sandflies. The choice was the stifling thick blanket of a mozzie net, or of being stung, risking bites so itchy they'd be scratched into non-healing ulcers. Like the Chinese workers who had laboured to clean the soiled laundry of the European settlers, grandmother stoked a fire to boil clothes in a big copper. When she did the washing you couldn't tell where the water ended and sweat began.

'I loved the heat. I just enjoyed working in boots and a hat, shorts, that's it,' Bill shrugs, when I press for more on 'the lived experience' of post-war Darwin and its contrast with his former life in Sydney. 'I never whinged about it.' The implied criticism of those that do hovers between us. I make a mental note about this thermal moralism, so characteristic of Darwinites and their nostalgia about the good old days before air-conditioning made everyone soft.

The heat! It turns up everywhere, in talk about rain that doesn't arrive and the sleep that swelter kills; in talk designed to evade talk about much at all. Heat, says anthropologist Michael Taussig, is like sound or colour: unrepresentable in its intensity. The breathlessness of it. The way it clots the air and makes pillows damp with sweat. Odd then, that this force which is most like drugs and dreams combined, all hallucinogenic and hammering, this primal condition beyond anyone's control, becomes the way of talking about banal things, a way of avoiding 'anything that would threaten the social bond for which weather talk is such a balm'.

For creased men with bloodshot eyes and heavy histories, moving beyond laconic phrases might also have dissolved the fragile threads holding them together. Drink was one glue; weather talk another. And for people in Darwin today, the heat binds strangers to old-timers, weather talk substituting for anything more difficult in high-turnover communities. Kind of like how the novelist Alexis Wright described how Aboriginal people are 'forced to hold much of their contact history with white people locked away inside of themselves', blood-soaked acts of dispossession not being part of safe talk. Weather talk smothers hardships, makes light of heavy things – for it was still a mean, hard town to live in.

Back when electricity was insufficient and air-conditioners not even a fantasy, people had different mechanisms for dealing with the build-up heat, the time when breezes are so mean-spirited they refuse to take sweat away. The Chinese had a contraption they nicknamed a Dutch wife, an aide not for sex but for airing the skin. Made of wicker or bamboo, this long, hollow tube removed the weight of sheets and stopped skin from self-adhering in hot, trickling body pockets. Embracing the wicker roll as one might spoon a lover, between arms and legs, the sleeper exposes her inner thighs and armpits to air. Sprays of water and wet hessian bags also helped.

Broken as it was, my grandparents were lucky to have any house at all. Just as it had been for the early settlers, there was little in the way of private accommodation, for the Commonwealth government had resumed all the freehold titles within the town one day after the war with Japan had officially ended. Returnees to Darwin had to contend with massive housing shortages, while those who owned property or businesses endured

bureaucratic procrastination and long corres-
pondence delays with faceless men in Canberra
before being permitted to rebid for their homes
and leases. It created almost total dependence on
government housing. Families were living in sub-
standard army huts; others had nothing at all. The
engineer George Redmond, who came to Darwin
to assume the position of head of the Department
of Works, had only one word to describe how he
felt about the situation: appalled. He was told by
his department superiors in Canberra that the
entire Northern Territory, not simply Darwin,
was so lacking in prospects no money could be
put aside for it. 'In the construction of government
houses, cost-saving measures were a dominant
consideration,' he later wrote. 'No hot water, no
doors to built-in wardrobes, no linoleum or vinyl
tiles for kitchens, bathrooms and toilets, and only
two ceiling fans were to be provided.' For toilets,
many householders still had 'flaming furies': holes
in the ground, kept level by being doused in kerosene and burnt every week. While yours was being
burnt, a neighbour's would need to be used, smoke
signals tom-tomming intimate news far and wide.

When Veronica Claverhouse-Dundee visited her daughter Frances, my mother, in the

prefabricated house my newlywed parents were then living in, she was so shocked she cut her trip short and headed back to Tasmania.

'It was all too much for her,' my mother explains. 'There were no overhead fans. We were pushing it to even have a bed. She thought it was just a terrible place. She said of Darwin, "Give it back to the blacks" – which is a very wise thing to say about the whole Territory, when I think back.' It's a good joke, thinking a Dundee from the House of Claver would come up with such a decolonising sentiment.

My parents were staying in what were known as Hawksleys, cheap prefabricated tin sheds with eight-foot-high ceilings, near today's Mantra Pandanus apartment tower in Darwin's CBD. Built on a cement slab, the original Hawksleys were not elevated and had no louvres for airflow. Even the distant Canberra administration had reservations about their suitability, as historian Mickey Dewar explains, but expediency won out. The demand for houses was so acute they decided that 'every house which was originally ordered for construction on behalf of the Administration, and which remains in crates, should be constructed'.

The 1950s resettlement of Darwin saw a new

population forging friendships in and through the heat, drinks in hand. There were characters with manners severe and undemonstrative until loosened by alcohol. Others, like the hook-handed deep-sea diver Carl Atkinson, whose fish-feeding habits at Doctors Gully created today's Aquascene tourist attraction, had loud eccentricities on full display. For young men and women the freedom was incomparable. You could ride motorbikes without a license, get drunk under-age, go fishing for days at a time, camp where you laid your swag. The army had made off with most things of value, but they left some good stuff behind too, in among the bullets and unexploded bombs. There were latrines and shower blocks. Men could decorate their homes with cattle horns and crocodile jaws. Army wire could be used to make fish traps. Among the fuel tanks was one reserved for water to douse fires, used as a secret pool. Nurses enjoyed the attentions of the men at the barracks, who would send cars over to collect the ladies for any dance or dinner, concocting events to avail themselves of female company. Kids plucked wild passionfruit from rampant vines, raided tamarind and cheeky plum trees, and ate sour rosella leaves until their stinging palates mutinied. Folk went swimming in creeks and billabongs, found breezy spots for picnics, met to drink iced liquids, made bets on anything that moved, enjoyed the fans at the open-air picture shows at the Star Theatre, sashayed at the Sunshine Club in Parap Camp or danced at the Hotel Darwin, depending on which track side they hailed from. And everywhere, there was bonding through the idle chitchat of weather talk.

Tocker Lea, Pop, never left. 'He nearly got out after Cyclone Tracy but he bailed up at the last minute. He never went further south than Berry Springs,' Bill tells me.

People often say that about the Territory: how they arrived temporarily then stayed put. In fact, alongside the astonishing flushing of people coming and going (approximately one quarter of the population between any census period), there is a worrisome minority of people who have literally never been anywhere else. I picture Appalachian stereotypes and feral pig shooters in Darwin's backblocks. More likely, the researchers tell me, they are just ordinary folk, like my old

Greek neighbours who feed their chickens, entertain an extended family and grow eggplants, happily shuffling through an unchanging routine, day after day.

'A wide bay appearing'

How did this place, of all places, get to be named after one of the greatest natural scientists of the western world? Given its transplanted socio-economic genesis, shouldn't Darwin have been named after some British dignitary or another, like all the other capital cities? After all, this is how it was originally named, when it was called Palmerston, after the British Prime Minister, infamous for savaging the Irish and inhabiting Parliament for almost his entire life.

For all its capacities for reinvention, it is Darwin's unique geology, and not its resilience, that lie behind its unique commemorative naming. HMS *Beagle* is renowned for its part in opening the wonders of the evolutionary world to the young naturalist, Charles Darwin, over the years 1831 to 1836. It was this ship, and some of Darwin's former shipmates, who connected Charles Darwin's geological interests with the interesting formations shaping Darwin's harbour.

The *Beagle* was then on its third circumnavigation, with its captain, John Wickham, and his lieutenant John Lort Stokes, sailing with instructions from the British Admiralty to settle, once and for all, whether or not there was an inland river. A river would make the massive Australian continent an easier country to extract wealth from, there was no doubt, and the search for it did not end until Matthew Flinders completed the charts in 1803 and died a broken man.

In the mild September heat of 1839, with the *Beagle* anchored elsewhere, a shore crew led by Stokes explored the Darwin harbour entrance, sleeping overnight on land. The morning brought a new discovery: 'Before the veil of darkness was quite removed, we could faintly distinguish the mouth of the opening; and the sight at daylight was most cheering. A wide bay appearing between white cliffy heads, and stretching away within to a great distance, presented itself to our view.'

As they clambered over rock faces, Stokes found his thoughts drifting with affection to their former shipmate, Charles Darwin. They named a headland Talc Head after the fine-grained siltstone and soft talc slate they found there. Rubbing the slippery grits between their fingers, they mused that this was just the sort of material the naturalist would have been excited by. In the habit of imperial Englishmen merging survey ventures and personal reveries with official naming systems, the contemplation 'afforded us an appropriate opportunity of convincing an old shipmate and friend that he still lived in our memory; and we accordingly named this sheet of water Port Darwin'.

Charles had secured a place in their affections as much through his incessant vomiting aboard the tiny *Beagle* as the methodical research that would make him one of the most famous scientists in Western history. He had shared the tiny poop cabin with Stokes and another survey officer for the full eighteen months of sea time in that historic five-year journey. And even though he never found his sea legs, his diligence impressed. Penning his obituary upon Darwin's death for the *London Times*, Stokes later wrote:

Perhaps no one can better testify to his early and most trying labours than myself. We worked together for several years at the same table in the poop cabin of the *Beagle* during her celebrated voyage, he with his microscope and myself at the charts. It was often a very lively end of the little craft, and distressingly so to my old friend, who suffered greatly from sea-sickness. After, perhaps, an hour's work he would say to me 'Old fellow, I must take the horizontal for it,' that being the best relief position for ship motion; a stretch out on one side of the table for some time would enable him to resume his labours for a while, when he again had to lie down.

For his part, it was memory of just how miserably unwell he could be at sea that prevented Darwin from travelling on the *Beagle* with Stokes ever again. Darwin the man never saw Darwin the place because of it. He had felt sicker in the final four months of his epic journey on the *Beagle* than he had at the beginning and later wrote, 'I loathe, I abhor the sea and all ships which sail on it. Not even the thrill of geology makes up for the misery and vexation of spirit that comes with sea-sickness.'

Even so, until overland travel could be secured with roads, bridges, train lines and air routes, ships were the lifeline for the place named after the land-hugging Charles Darwin. It was a world defined by water: swamps, monsoon rains, rivers and things borne by waters that promise and trick, nourish and kill. The Larrakia and other Aboriginal groups in the region found it much easier to get around than the Europeans. They burnt the spear grass during the Dry Season and used dugout and bark canoes to navigate the monsoonal wetlands, storing their vessels in the higher mangroves in between journeys.

In contrast, the settlers battled the tangled thickets and sank their drays in the swamps. During the Top End's short-lived gold rush, brought on by the discovery of gold at Yam Creek (about 140 kilometres south-east of Darwin), hundreds of men came to seek their fortune. Offloading in wharfless Darwin, they immediately faced the challenge of transport. It took '41 days to travel a distance which, in the 1870s, normally took three days during the Dry season'. It was impossible to rupture the fortune seekers' faith in the superiority of their technologies: native techniques for being fleet-footed were never mimicked. Chinese labourers and carting animals were conscripted instead. And by the time stray buffalo, pigs, horses, cats and dogs had purposefully or accidentally been let loose within the region, the natural banks separating salt from freshwater marshes became so damaged that moving overland became a battle with disease-bearing mosquitoes, populations of which thrived even more in the brackish inland deltas. To the smallpox and measles epidemics that swept through Aboriginal groups across Australia, on top of bullets, forced migrations and indenturing, came attacks from the alien diseases carried by mosquitoes. Malaria, introduced by settlers and their trading partners, killed Aboriginal people during the settlement period in unknown numbers. Unknown and unknowable – for they were never counted – yet devastating, for malaria is not a disease of nomads but of people crowded into the one place.

The lands surrounding Darwin Harbour did not look promising to Stokes, who followed his eulogies about the bay with less sanguine observations. He wrote of the 'annoyance' of mosquitoes and sandflies, of 'alligators' in the harbour that 'swarmed in dangerous numbers' and of the 'thirsty-looking country' up on higher land. Beyond the mangroves came 'low brushwood … which cracked and snapped as we walked through it, with a brittle dryness that testified how perfectly parched-up was everything', matched by 'slight blasts of heated withering air, as if from an oven, [that] would occasionally strike the face as we walked along'. Concluding, he noted: 'There was nothing of interest to recall our memories to this first visit to a new part of Australia, save a very large ant's nest, measuring twenty feet in height. This object is always the first that presents itself whenever my thoughts wander to that locality.'

Yet this was the site chosen by the Surveyor-General of South Australia, George Woodroffe Goyder, for the settlement of Darwin. The South Australian government had annexed the Northern Territory in 1863 as part of the scramble to divide the continent among state colonies. By exaggerating the strategic significance of the port in relation to trade with Asia, its agricultural potential and the opportunities for sheep and cattle runs, they helped create the first of the manufactured real estate frenzies that have helped buoy the Darwin economy on and off ever since. Determined to make an 'inexpensive penetration', the government marketed the future capital as a site for Australia's next bonanza, its allotments sold off a nonexistent survey plan to absent speculators in Adelaide and

London. It would be six years before Goyder could actually survey the land that was pre-sold; and less than fifty years before the South Australians could divest themselves of their bad investment.

Darwin's climate and geological intractability have ensured it remains Australia's smallest capital city. Its serial destructions have seen the question 'Why Darwin?' officially revisited multiple times in its short history. Men – they were always men – have sat around boardroom tables and pondered the challenge; politicians have debated in parliaments; commissions of inquiry have reported their considered verdicts. Each time the answer calls upon a form of geographical determinism. Because of where it is located, trade with Asia is assured. One way or another, money can be extracted from the land and sea. There are development opportunities in mining, pastoralism and agriculture, the men kept saying, seldom matching the spin with serious capital investment or sustained expertise. And of course, they would add, as if in afterthought, the country needs to guard its north.

I see it differently. Darwin is sculpted by four

major forces. The first is geological. The town is based on a skinny peninsula barely rising above drowned river valleys that are slowly filling with silt. Suitable land is scarce and it is an ongoing, energy-intensive struggle to make the place habitable. The second is ecological. The humble mosquito killed off the first three attempts at northern settlement and drives conditions for the built environment to this day. Climate and isolation foster the population turnover and underpin the high costs of living. Third, it is a garrison town, a fact that is hidden in plain sight. Meeting Defence needs has periodically been the pump used to aspirate Darwin's inflatable bop-bag resurrections. And finally, it is founded on Aboriginal land, a fact that cannot be conveniently footnoted into past history, but explains the mix, socially, politically and economically, that makes up Darwin.

In everyday life, these forces morph and merge in confounding, intoxicating ways. For all the upheaval, post-war immigration energised Darwin as it did elsewhere, with new generations of settlers, waves of Greeks and Italians, followed in later decades by Vietnamese, Timorese and Filipinos, who renovated the town again. Darwin's architecture and urban design reflect the marks different sojourners stamp with every metamorphosis. Like the wounds from its devastations, each makeover is ephemeral; or, more accurately, heritage needs to be glimpsed in scattered and elusive material remains. The place has an Ozymandian quality: buildings, furniture, appliances do not survive long. Even the dumping grounds of Nightcliff, where unwanted machinery and detritus from World War II were tipped over a cliff, have merged into the rocks below, no longer distinguishable, just deformed lumps of rust and chalk.

The environmental battles have yielded today's whole-of-yard house designs that use concrete besser blocks, sliding glass windows and cement rendering to create hermetically sealed McMansions. Contemporary Darwin is as much an ode to the powers of air conditioning and engineering as it is an ongoing lesson in the folly of trying to bend the biosphere to settlement will. The pressures of catering for an expanding population in the face of land shortages also gives rise to houses that kill. The toxic melioidosis bacterium lives dormant in the soil until brought to the surface by earthworks and rain, causing pneumonia and septicaemia. Its incidence is rising with each new subdivision as the population expands. The turquoise waters of the Timor Sea are hazardous with prehistoric crocodiles and, as reliable as the build-up, become a beckoning sea that repels human entry by order of the most venomous creature on earth: the box jellyfish, *Chironex fleckeri*, increasing in numbers as the water warms and acidifies.

There are battles with introduced cane toads. Hire cars and government fleet vehicles have stickers warning drivers to immediately remove bat splats, lest the paintwork corrode down to the metal. Even the famed tropical sunsets are made more intense by smoke particles from burning gamba grass, a species introduced for feeding cattle that even four-wheel drive vehicles can't knock down. Servicing Aboriginal people has not only created unique postcolonial industries, it explains why Northern Territory citizens receive generous financial loadings from the Common-wealth – loadings which make up 80 per cent of the Territory budget.

The military gave Darwin the Stuart Highway, bridging in one season the 630-mile gap that work undertaken sporadically since 1886 on the north-south transcontinental railway had left undone. Defence built one of Australia's largest runways;

it gave the town a vital post-cyclone population boost, housing finances, money for road repairs and swamp drainage, a larger than usual sex industry and more besides, including fighter jets with high-thrust engines exploding into the air. And the historic Leanyer Air Weapons Range created a 90-hectare area of bomb craters — marvellously productive breeding sites for disease-bearing varieties of salt marsh mosquitoes.

It is a tough, fragile, magical, hilarious, foolhardy and unique town, its policy foibles offset by its rich cultural history and humbling wild beauty. Once known as Australia's Little Moscow in light of its working class activism, it is also deeply politically conservative. Famed for its hunting, shooting, fishing and drinking 'Territory lifestyle', its many sojourners also live in fearful tension with the place they are in. Helpers who come to change Aboriginal people end up changed themselves. There is a unique humour and matching vocabulary, part creolised, that makes Darwinites instantly recognisable to each other — that's no gammon. Insiders give outsiders a citizen test: a pass/fail based on the unique salty plum. To the aficionado these red, brown or grey dried prunes, preserved Chinese-style in salt, liquorice and sweeteners, are a delicious snack and cure-all. They can be eaten any time and are just the thing for a sore throat. Sadly, too many test subjects spit out these delightful lumps of chewy brine, scraping their tongues forcefully against their upper teeth to scour the taste away.

Such a waste of a good salty plum.

2

Dangerous proximities

Hooves and guns

By the closing decade of the 19th century, the South Australian Minister for Education and the Northern Territory, Sir Frederick Holder, advised his colleagues to retract the South Australian border to the MacDonnell Ranges and yield the rest of the Northern Territory back to the mother country. The British politely declined. After a decade of bickering, by 1911 the Northern Territory became a responsibility of the Commonwealth government – its status to this day. The

Territory's limited self-government was bestowed in 1978 as an Act of the Australian parliament, and its deliberations as a government can still be overturned at the stroke of a pen.

The year 1911 ended the disastrous, violent South Australian rule. Yet while disappointed land-order owners had found no bonanza from their distant speculations, the time of absentee landlords was far from over. At this point, Darwin had the bare outlines of a European settlement. More a shanty town than a capital city, it was made up of a telegraph line connecting Port Augusta to Port Darwin and thence to the British Empire, a changing mix of Aboriginal people, and a thrifty and industrious Chinese population who so threatened Anglo-Australian self-assurance that the White Australia policy was unleashed. The frontiersmen who came to the district included cattle and horse thieves, outlaws, divers, capitalists, dreamers, drunks, schemers — men escaping their own histories and out to transgress the wilderness. The traditional estates of Aboriginal people from Darwin to the Northern Territory borders and beyond were harnessed to the dreams of fortune seekers and the speculations of men in other towns and continents. The traditional owners of the Darwin region, the Larrakia, survived this and more, to the point where, uniquely in Australia, Aboriginal people now determine the electoral fate of the Northern Territory government, and the Larrakia Development Corporation – the economic arm of the Northern Land Council – is a major real estate developer in its own right.

Cattle have been part of Darwin's story from the beginning. It had been pastoralists who urged the South Australian annexation of the north in the first place, hoping to cater for the ever-elusive Asian market. A massive pastoral invasion across the top half of the Northern Territory was triggered by favourable reports from explorers. As they continued to sail the HMS *Beagle* around the north Australian coast, Wickham and Stokes also continued to explore and name the Top End's inland rivers. Their promising descriptions of the Victoria River in particular led to Augustus Charles Gregory's exploratory expedition, first by boat, then on horse and on foot, paving the way for the Territory's famed pastoral runs.

For Aboriginal people, the pastoral invasion

was brutal and unrelenting. Darwin encompassed the traditional lands of people belonging to the Larrakia language group, but in the early days of the settlement, refugees from outside Darwin also moved to the new town. They were called 'outsiders' and 'myalls' then, when the land was still being fought for; and 'long-grassers' and 'itinerants' today, now land fights are conducted with the scissor-hand of legal contracts. During the long wars of resistance and punishment, stockmen were paid extra for being 'hard on blacks' and teaching 'lessons' — euphemisms for wholesale slaughter on the quasi-legal pretext cattle had been speared.

This is how erasures begin, with allusive words and details left unspecified. 'Punishment also involved wanton destruction. After slaughtering the occupants of a camp, the police and others would burn the bodies, homes, weapons and canoes, and shoot the dogs.' Makes you wonder whose life was wilder, that of the hunter–gatherer trying to eat, or the hard men who shot at them, burning and burying evidence as they went? As Tony Roberts describes it:

> In 1881, a massive pastoral boom commenced
> in the top half of the Northern Territory,

administered by the colonial government in Adelaide. Elsey Station on the Roper River – romanticised in Jeannie Gunn's *We of the Never Never* – was the first to be established. These were huge stations, with an average size of almost 16 000 square kilometres. By the end of the year the entire Gulf district (an area the size of Victoria, which accounted for a quarter of the Territory's pastoral country) had been leased to just 14 landholders, all but two of whom were wealthy businessmen and investors from the eastern colonies.

Their visions were part the wish fulfilment of hard men throwing their bodies into dramatic and dangerous places, part straight ignorance of the tropical savanna and its insistent refusal of Eurocentric templates for socioeconomic development. How else could the potential of the 'wide bay appearing' bear fruit, if riches from the hinterland were not generated to cart through it? People from cattle cultures know few other ways. The leaseholders had only three years to comply with the minimum stocking rates; only three years to clear the land of its competitors, be it the Aboriginal families who walked their estates or the native fauna and flora.

Wholesale pastoral settlement required the rapid emptying of territory. It was a zero-sum equation.

There is little recorded about what the Larrakia and other groups said among themselves about the new interlopers in this early period. What did they make of a people who protected their rights to stolen property with guns and jails for want of a reciprocal system of asking and sharing? Matching the colonisers as masters of understatement, the sudden, violent frontier is 'remembered in Aboriginal English variously as "the killing times", "the quietening time" and "station times"'.

Between the killings there were robbings, humiliations, rapes and jailings. There was gambling, and trade in alcohol at the backs of pubs and down alleyways. And there was sex. So many men, so few women. Racial segregation, so rigidly upheld in some places, was observed in the breach in others. Compassion and intimacy leavened the hostility. The wonder of it is that out of all this comes the old families of Darwin and their deep friendships across racial lines. Lovers stayed together in defiance of written and tacit laws. Families became interrelated, many proudly so. And out on the sports field, teams formed which respected speed, agility, marksmanship and group work, regardless of ethnic identity or class allegiance. Yet nostalgia about these bonds is also a way that Darwinites make themselves innocent of the town's dormant divisions.

Along with tried and failed tobacco, breadfruit, rice and sugar cane crops, sheep and cattle herds were attempted. Sheep runs followed John McDouall Stuart's epic inland route, but the sheep died. Like cooked bones in a dog's gut, spear grass seeds pierced the sheep's bowel linings. The sheep starved during droughts, ate poisonous plants; the lambs suffered heat stress in the wet and died; the ewes were in too poor a condition to suckle during the dry.

No animal liberation protesters were around to deplore the prolonged and painful endings. Instead, like so many temperate enterprise dreams for the monsoon country, the desire to have sheep stations took a long time to be defeated. They were still being attempted when I was a little girl, out at Berrimah on Darwin's fringe. The CSIRO's scrawny, diseased-looking flocks predicted the 'Seedy Ewe' T-shirts created by postgraduate students at Charles Darwin University in 2003, lampooning the institution's name change from Northern Territory University, or NTU, to its new acronym, CDU.

In the meantime, the water buffalo which had first accompanied Major John Campbell to the ill-fated settlement of Fort Dundas on Melville Island ended up wild on the Alligator River flood plains, helping to create a sporadic industry in hides and horns from the early 1890s to the collapse of the hide market in the mid-1950s.

Cattle fared better. They fixed the image of the rugged stockman as the icon of the northern frontier, despite the wrenching cycles of boom and bust, changes of ownership and multiple closures that eventually made cattle the business of absentee robber barons who held the largest runs, such as Bovril and then the Vestey Brothers.

In 1914, Bovril's north Australian holdings were the largest in the British empire. Two years later, they were eclipsed by the Union Cold Storage Company, aka Vestey Brothers. When Vesteys added Wave Hill Station to their estates elsewhere in Australia and Argentina, they became the largest meat company in the world. The cattle kings were as important to the financing of global capital as mining conglomerates, the narcotics industry and military suppliers are today, their cattle as good as armed tanks for taking land, as thorough as strip miners for environmental damage. They also stunted the north for decades, with Aborigines at the lethal end of a long exploitation line.

Like the founders of Bovril, brothers William and Edmund Vestey capitalised on global war to dominate the meat market, aggressively buying out rivals or displacing them from the market, avoiding tax and – like drug dealers – disguising the ownership of their companies in dense financial tributaries. They were the first to take advantage of new refrigeration technologies to freight perishable food across large distances. They owned the cold storage facilities, the shipping lines, the wholesale and the retail outlets down to the level of the butcher, across a global beef supply chain. They could suppress wages where and as they liked, close and open operations as and when it suited, muscle out competition and control a country's development. They were also, according to investigative journalist Nicholas Shaxson, 'pioneers of today's global tax avoidance industry' – and ecological vandals to boot.

Throwing open the Northern Territory to the

Vestey and Bovril empires did little for animal husbandry or station improvement. The companies did not invest in their holdings beyond the crudest of measures, but degraded the best of the cattle country at microscopic rentals, paid little to no tax on profits from their holdings and benefited from Aboriginal slave labour. And through mythologisation and boosterism, continuing to this day via provincial historians, the cattle barons were able to represent their interests as aligned with those of the public at large.

I went to Darwin High School, a pragmatic building on a piece of cliff known as Bullocky Point, wedged between Mindil Beach and the shores of Fannie Bay. The school comprised a pair of elongated grey rectangular blocks, each two storeys high, named gulag-style as A and B block, linked by a glass-walled gangway. The spectacular views were blighted by the always grimy windows and dented awnings, while navigating the run between lessons was an exercise in battling bottlenecks on crowded stairwells and crashing through double doors into long linoleum-covered corridors. The school has since had a number of makeovers and is today an elite institution, the closest to a selective public secondary facility the Northern Territory offers. It sits on the exact site of Vestey's meat-processing plant at Bullocky Point, built by the multinational company in 1914, opened for business in 1917 and closed by way of telegraph order from Lord Vestey four years later.

It would have been possible, even then, to link cattle to markets with railway communications and freezing facilities, but the large pastoral companies also opposed railways for their habit of splitting their large estates. The railway would have to wait. Instead, with absentee landholders, disinvestment, a license to indenture Aboriginal labour as inmates and cattle station managers with, might we say, *varying* moralities, cattle were moved by drovers. The hungry soldiers swarming the north following the Japanese bombing created a local market out of the inefficient northern pastoral industry – and the frontier legends began.

As I interviewed Bill Lea, his story shifted from warfare to droving. Leaving Darwin, as young people in the mid-1950s had to do to complete their secondary education, my father was sent to live with relatives in Sydney. He excelled at mathematics, enough to win state and Common-wealth-sponsored civil engineering scholarships at the University of Sydney. But with no home desk to study at, long commutes, the pain of working-class self-consciousness within an elite institution and bronchial infections that saw him coughing blood at the start of each confronting day, he gave university away six months in. Freedom as a Northern Territory bushman beckoned.

In 1953, as a still-green drover, Bill was hired as part of a team to muster 1350 head of stock, shifting them from Coolibah Station in the Victoria River Downs across the swollen flood plains of the Barkly Tablelands to Delmore Downs, over 700 miles (1100 kilometres) away. The team had been contracted by Delmore's leaseholders, a sub-sidiary of the Tom Piper Food Company, which had bought Delmore as a virgin block with no cattle. The company had advanced £12 500 to Leslie John Kenna to help him buy Coolibah Station. Bill's droving run was a form of debt collection.

Kenna's debt was to be repaid by way of 8000 cattle, delivered over several years from Coolibah to Delmore. Several shipments had already been made; only two more were required to clear the debt. In a separate deal, Kenna's station manager, one Hugh Wason Byers, would become an equal partner in Coolibah once the debt was extinguished. Byers was thus keen to settle the account, but he knew Kenna had signed them both up to a tight deal of delivering stock they didn't really have.

The droving was hard. A mixed herd of over 1350 head had been mustered for the partial repayment: cleanskins and branded cattle, bullocks and cows all in together. The riders needed to work in shifts, day and night, circling the herds to keep birthing cows from breaking out and aroused bulls from breaking in.

'With droving you have horses that can do night watches and others for the day,' Bill said. 'It was us people who did the double shifts. That droving trip I was on a horse seventeen hours a day and sometimes more, for five and half months.'

Whenever a cow gave birth, the calf was immediately killed and the mother forced back into the herd, for grief would bind her to the death site. The drovers would use the surge of the herd to force her from the great wrenching loss of her newborn.

'Did you eat them?' I ask, naively.

'No, they're rubbish – no flesh, all bones. You just hit 'em on the head and worry about the cow.'

It was the end of the wet and the rivers were still high. The wild cattle resist the rising waters and throw their heads back, straining their eyes and stamping their hooves in terror. They have to be forced across fast waters. The rivers turn the black soil country of the Barkly into glutinous mud. The horses get swamp cancer, an ulcerous fungal infection that thrives in heat and humidity. Cattle break their legs in unseen potholes.

'We lost one horse in the big, swollen rivers. Lost our sugar and salt that way too. That whole country is full of rivers.

'Salt is your fridge. When you kill a bullock, most of it you salt and dry. I had a rifle which the cook lost in the bloody river too. We had no way of keeping the meat and we no longer had a gun to shoot it. So we had to throw an animal every day and stick a knife in the back of its neck. We killed one every day. I got fat eating their kidneys; no one else liked them, so I ate them by myself, all full of fat.'

Bill smacks his lip with the memory.

Any time the rain let up, the men tried to air their swags, flicking out accumulating maggots

breeding in the dank pockets of sweat and lukewarm animal blood. They were moving the mixed
herd from Coolibah Station down through Skull
Creek. A deep killing poison pulses through this
back country. Skull Creek got its name after the
Barrow Creek massacre of 1874, when up to ninety
Kaytetye – men, women and children – were murdered, their skulls left to bleach in the desert sun.
Later, it was the police station manager from
Barrow Creek who led the posse for the Coniston
massacre in 1928, officially the last sanctioned
slaughter of Aborigines in Australia.

As they approached a rendezvous point for a
scheduled stock inspection, not that far out from
Victoria River Downs Station, the head drover
Billy Ellis leant back in his saddle, nodded his
chin forward. A spartan prophecy: 'There'll be
trouble up ahead.'

Ellis knew that some of the cattle had been
rebranded and that cleanskins had been recently
marked. Bovril's station manager, sent to inspect
the shipment as it went along its way, spied the
fresh marks and let the police in on his suspicions.
The plant kept droving, their herd intact, all the
way to Anthony Lagoon, where the coppers showed
up again. The police corralled 104 head, shooting

and killing some to use in evidence, throwing the hides over a fence to dry.

Seems Byers had stolen cattle from Victoria River Downs Station, then owned by Bovril Australian Estates, to pad out the Coolibah's debt repayment, and Bovril wanted their cattle back. VRD's well-known bull's head cattle brand had been covered with Coolibah's MTQ and hand brands, using solid blocks rather than an outline to disguise the original marks. Block brands not only disguise cattle duffing, they can burn the cattle so severely their skin peels away in cruel patches. That is one way duffing can be identified. Haste can also share secrets. Sometimes the rebranding had been done so hurriedly the tips of two horns still showed.

Byers was a cold man, renowned in a country inured to racial terror as particularly brutal with blacks. The filmmakers Charles and Elsa Chauvel had used Coolibah Station to film parts of the movie *Jedda*, the first full-length colour feature film using Aboriginal actors ever made in Australia. They had even found a bit part for Byers to play, as head drover. As the 'son of a grazier turned light-horseman', Humphrey McQueen notes, Charles Chauvel 'had a personal commitment to the settlement tradition … of tough men sticking by their mates, at pioneering or at war'. Charles liked Byers and called him Felix Romeo in the movie. But to his wife and fellow producer Elsa, their talent was 'a bully and at times rather sadistic'. Byers, she would record in her memoirs, was

> a rough-hewn man, moody and aggressive … who used to delight in giving me the horrors at the dinner table. He would glare at me and his great monster of a clenched fist would come down with a crash on the rough wooden table like an exploding bomb, lifting the knives and forks a foot high and scattering them.

The tough man liked to use his whip and his gun to teach his lessons. He told historian Pearl Ogden how he hated the sound of the didgeridoo going from morning to night. 'When one bugger knocks up, another will take it on,' he complained. Whistling, yelling, cracking a whip – even blasting a gun did nothing to shut the songmen up. He tried a new tactic:

> [so] this bloke, this Congal, I said 'Did you play that didgeridoo last night?' and he said yes. So

I said, 'All right, you bring em one down.' I said,
'You get up that pole, that post in the yard, and
you play that didgeridoo.' Every time he stopped
playing, I'd fire a shot at him. Well, he kept
playing that didgeridoo, playing all day ... I never
heard a bloody didgeridoo for months after.

Byers laughs, Ogden wrote, as he tells her this.

Edgar Laytha, a freelancing American journalist
who travelled with the Darwin Overland Maintenance Force in 1941 as it cut the future Stuart
Highway, also met Byers on his travels and thought
him 'a magnificent figure, with the face of a man
who had been through everything'. Somewhat pro-
phetically, Laytha had written a piece for the *Saturday Evening Post*, a prestigious New York magazine,
describing the inevitability of a Japanese attack on
Britain's next safest port: Darwin. He had spent
several years in Japan before the war, and had read
Japanese navy Lieutenant-Commander Ishimaru's
book *Japan Must Fight Britain*, which detailed exactly
what the British would need to do if attacked.
Anticipating the geographic ignorance of his

American readers, Laytha reminded them that the Japanese knew the seas between Australia, Indonesia and Timor better than the Europeans. After all, they had been sending fishing and pearling luggers there for years, often captained by naval reserve officers.

With all this in his background, Laytha was particularly interested in what he called 'Australia's baby Singapore', becoming one of two American journalists to report from the inland Australian front as the Stuart Highway was finally sealed. The intrepid journalist finds a way to let the readers know something else: unlike his colleague from *National Geographic Magazine*, who preferred the padded comfort of a private car, Laytha shared the road with the convoys, camping roadside with workers at night and eating in their mess tents. He liked these men who worked through an 'inferno of heat and drought' to build Australia's Burma Road at record speed. He liked their grit, their work ethic, their sense of humour. The only thing breaking the 'deadening monotony' of the hot, dusty space they worked through – 'infinity to the right, infinity to the left, infinity ahead and infinity behind' – were the bores at 50-mile (80-kilometre) intervals (mostly former Aboriginal watering holes), and the talk of the men.

It was during one of these stops that Laytha found himself charmed by the laconic wisecracks of Hugh Wason Byers, finding in him the same outback spirit he so admired in the army men. Laytha had come Australia to learn more about this young country which as recently as 1939 'had depended upon the rest of the world for its technology', the newest democracy in the Pacific. In the shortest of times, he told his American readers, Australians have 'organized and equipped from their own newly built factories a complete armored division ... carrying out at the same time a huge ship, plane and munitions-making program' and put 'in uniform nearly 40 per cent of all her men from nineteen to thirty-nine'. This was a country which could and would defend Darwin against the Japanese, for even now the men were champing at the bit for action, having headed to Darwin supposing they would embark for Singapore.

Laytha's leading article sits among hand-drawn advertisements identifying a confident America: life insurance for men who work and dream and plan for the future, Whitman's chocolates, Formfit undergarments and Chevrolet cars. There is even an innovation from the Dow Chemical Company — headed today by one of Darwin's most successful live exports, Andrew Liveris — an ice tray with removable plastic cups. With only the slightest of pressure, the mixer of cold beverages for home consumption can take as many ice cubes as needed, one by itself or the whole dozen.

In the time between writing and publication, Singapore fell. And five days after Laytha's article was posted, Darwin was annihilated.

Dad tells me Byers had served in World War I as a light horseman and would have held his own as a raconteur when the highway workers passed through. His fearsome reputation among Aboriginal people, in a country known for its brutality, would have been no barrier to bush mateship. He had the sangfroid of the law flouter, the amoral edge that can be so attractive to those whose interests are being tacitly served by outlier barbarity, a hint of the raw cruelty lurking beyond the mannered hospitality of whitefellas. He was rumoured to have 'ant-hilled' Aboriginal men to even a score, letting meat ants take care of the murdered remains.

One time, Bill tells me, Byers had come back to Coolibah to find that the vegetable garden had not been watered or the water tanks not kept full – people can't seem to remember which and historians haven't trapped the offending detail.

'So he made the lubras strip to nothing and got them to sit on the hot tin roof, whipping them to shift to the next more blazing spot,' says Dad.

'Wason wasn't at the [cattle duffing] trial,' Bill continues, 'but we heard later that he got word to the blackfellas that if they dobbed him in, he would do 'em. He got off, but he lost that station eventually and drank rum and told stories. See that book – you know, that one who reckons he's the real Crocodile Dundee. Tom Cole. *Hell, West and Crooked*. He goes into it.'

I don't need to read the story filtered through the ripping yarns of retired bushmen, with their softened terms for the pastoral killing fields. The story Bill Lea tells me seems incredible but the always partial archives bear him out. It was the biggest case of alleged cattle rustling ever to go to trial in the Northern Territory; it was heard by a Supreme Court judge, Martin Kriewaldt. The journalist Douglas Lockwood covered the bush court and it was reported across the country.

Byers was charged with ten counts of stealing ninety head of oxen, cows, heifers and calves. The court was held on the verandah of Anthony's Lagoon police station, over 43 degrees Celsius in the shade, over a long, hot week. Judge Kriewaldt sat in red fur-fringed robes and wool wig in the blistering heat. Ringers, head stockmen and drovers sat in the gallery. Three Aboriginal station hands from Coolibah — Duncan, Hector and Bloomer — gave evidence. Even the cattle who had performed so well for *Jedda*'s station scenes were made to testify. The crown prosecutor showed the inverted hides from the slaughtered beasts, the original VRD burns clear for all to see. As for Byers, he was defended by a silk flown in by light aircraft all the way from Adelaide.

There were several ways the flash QC could discredit the Aboriginal witnesses. He chose the uniformity of their testimony. With theatrical gestures, he turned to the gallery every now and again, appealing to their casually shared ethnocentrism, as he press-ganged Duncan and Bloomer into admitting perhaps they'd not seen much after all. Could it be they were simply repeating learnt lines?

Byers was acquitted.

I think of this trial and how it might proceed today. It is not the travelling Magistrates Courts and the haphazard use of translators that come to mind. Nor the attempts to have Aboriginal customary justice recognised within the property scripts known as Australian law. Instead, I think of the cattle and the under-resourced offices of the Northern Territory Ombudsman.

Carolyn Richards came into her role as Ombudsman in mid-2005 and was replaced by the incoming Country Liberal Party in late 2012. As Ombudsman she inquired into complaints received about the condition of the Brahman cattle at Mataranka Station, owned and managed by Charles Darwin University and used for training students who want to work on the land. Sometime between about August and December 2009 an estimated 800 cattle and horses died or were put down because of malnutrition and lack of water. Inspectors found tick-infested livestock with bones jagging their hides, some so sick meat ants were killing them as they stood. Toby Gorringe, a university vocational trainer, complained up the line, all the way to the Ombudsman. She wrote a report recommending prosecution, but no one was charged. With the assistance of government foot-dragging, the small 12-month window for bringing a charge under the *Animal Welfare Act* had expired.

Should there be any mistaking Darwin's ongoing kinship with the fortunes of the cattle industry, consider the impact of another truth-telling woman, Lyn White. This former police-woman turned animal activist had smuggled graphic footage of Australian cattle being tormented in an Indonesian abattoir, their eyes gouged and bodies slashed with blunt knives. Reporters from the Australian Broadcasting Commission's *Four Corners* program investigated for themselves. The initially low-rating 'A Bloody Business' became one of the biggest media stories of 2011. The *Four Corners* exposé unleashed such a furious public reaction the Australian government also reacted, by placing an immediate ban on exporting live cattle to Indonesia.

Driving from Darwin to Sydney in June 2011, camping in dusty outback towns along the way, the late autumn roads were gloriously empty of tourists. But joining me on the journey south were long lines of cattle trucks – the vehicles that had killed off the drovers and created a new breed of long-distance herder, the truckie – carrying loads of exhausted, frightened cattle. All heading in the wrong direction. The live export protest zeroed in on Indonesian killing techniques. Good abattoir practice, it was insisted, sees cattle stunned before they are knifed. Stunning makes an animal easier to handle, reducing its struggle, stopping cattle from manifesting the distress that proved so disturbing for Australian viewers. With Indonesian practices positioned as inhumane, Australian slaughterhouses were elevated, and the intensive farming practices that allow Australians to enjoy cheap meat left unframed.

Cattle-breeder and fourth-generation Darwinite Laurence Ah Toy gave me a similar reason for why buffalo are not exported live since the live export ban, despite the clear Asian preference for their meat. A stunning gun able to penetrate the buffalo's thicker skull has not yet been invented. Moreover, buffalo will stand and face a stockman or a dog rather than retreat into flight mode and move away, as cattle tend to do. And while buffalo can be trained to perform circus-type acts, they prefer being worked with a quieter, less confrontational approach. Nor do they like being crowded into confined spaces. All this makes them less popular along nodes of the export industry, from trucking and shipping and on to slaughter. Buffaloes more readily collapse the idea of humane killing into its oxymoron. Cattle, docility and stupefaction are preferred, to help make what is happening more appealing to humans.

Could this be a metaphor for Darwin's cultural and economic foundations? Not as the romantic pageant imagined by Baz Luhrmann's *Australia* – a panorama of mystical Aborigines, untamed outback men and pretty English damsels – but this insistence on remaining 'in a state of numbed indifference and ignorance to that which *we know not to know*?' In neo-colonial settings like Darwin, forgetting is a necessary kind of cultural habit, a social amnesia that helps the town cohere. It is the rough and the fancy coinciding that newcomers note, like watching the fabulous sunset at Mindil Beach to the raw sounds of a drunken feud. It is riding a bike path past a splay of homeless bodies. To live in a place where life does not stay sanitised for too long, where fantasies of urbane sophistication melt under the sticky glare of everyday realities, Darwinites learn to hover between knowing and ignoring. It makes them less easy with categorical distinctions between good and bad ethnicity, happy or habitual drunkenness, right and wrong animal deaths. It is a place which insists on mixing things up.

Flying darts

Before Darwin was built and destroyed four times over, four earlier attempts at coastal settlement had also cruelly foundered. The first was at Fort Dundas on Melville Island. The second was Fort Wellington on Raffles Bay. The township of Victoria in the doomed Port Essington, some 300 kilometres north-east of Darwin, was the third. These were all British. The fourth settlement was a South Australian one, the first Palmerston at Escape Cliffs. Each had been promoted on its outstanding merits.

The Reverend John Dunmore Lang described Port Essington as:

> a harbour second only to Port Jackson, and
> beyond all comparison, the best yet discovered
> on the north coast of the Australian continent
> … unquestionably one of the most commanding

positions for British settlement, whether in a
commercial, in a political, or in a moral and
religious light, on the face of the globe.

Like current promotions of The North as Australia's future food and water source, these optimistic
statements are almost comic in their omissions.
Port Essington was essentially a garrison town
manned almost exclusively by marines. The settlement site of Victoria, within Port Essington's
'best yet' harbour, was approachable only at high
tide, and sat too far from the open sea to catch
any of its breezes. It was all but wiped out by a
cyclone a year into its existence. Termites ate the
men's books and charts. Flies plagued their days;
mosquitoes haunted their nights. They filled the
enervating space of heat and boredom with such
petty feuds and caballing that writing of it later,
T.H. Huxley thought Port Essington 'about the
most useless, miserable, ill-managed hole in her
Majesty's dominion'. Four years after it was first
established, a malaria outbreak killed or invalided
half the garrison.

These were not easy deaths. The severest form
of malaria grips a person in a fever so bad it spins
their eyes apart. It inflames the brain until the

skull becomes a vice. Within as little as nine days, a person's blood cells start rupturing. Some die quickly; some take weeks, coming in and out of fever, lucidity bringing consciousness of dying – if not today, then soon.

Lassitude claimed what malaria did not, the men becoming so unbearably bored they simply wanted to die. Some drank so much they could only see darkness as they lay in the mud and accepted its microbial embrace. With their immune systems as paralysed as their bodies, the melioidosis bacteria crept in through cuts and gashes. Drunken stupor one day; poisoned blood the next. (The disease remains a killer of people living rough in the long grass – alcoholic oblivion, open sores and ground contact with bacteria the grave-digging nexus). The imagined coffee, sugar cane, sago and cotton plantations never emerged.

Undeterred, twenty years after the Port Essington experiment, Darwin (nee Palmerston) was established further to the west, where it still 'stands in splendid isolation, the only port city in half the circumference of Australia', the fifth attempt to establish a European settlement on the north Australian coast. The battle with mosquitoes was far from over.

Where the introduced communicable diseases of colonists operated as a 'microbial sword' in decimating previously isolated Indigenous populations, the disease-bearing mosquito was far more democratic. It targeted Aboriginal groups and settlers alike, indifferent to whether target populations had enforced or voluntary sedentarism. Animals also suffer. Within the hundred or so different mosquito species in the Northern Territory (of the 300 or so nationwide), some have a crude bite designed to get through a thick animal hide. Dogs get heartworm and frill-necked lizards a sickening parasite, while biting midges give livestock bluetongue and bovine ephemeral fever, which, left unchecked, threaten the live cattle trade as assuredly as any failure to stun animals pre-slaughter.

Mosquitoes pass their short but vital life in four key stages: from eggs to delicious larvae into pupae and thence to precision flyers. In less than a week of hatching, a mosquito will be able to fly with such split-second acumen it can manoeuvre around raindrops, with the instinctive good sense to avoid the cannonball run of a heavy thunderstorm. Scanning the field of blood before it with its inbuilt infrared vision and profound sense of smell, the female harvester can isolate the fine scent of carbon dioxide, the telltale sign of a warm-blooded animal, from a distance of around 50 metres, the length of an Olympic pool. Fine hunters all, the stealthiest is the female *Aedes aegypti*, carrier of dengue and the now rare yellow fever, whose stylets are so fine she can barely be felt. Where the males buzz loudly, she is silent, preferring humans above all mammals for her blood meals.

The mosquito is also a powerful urban planner, having shaped the spatial contours of Darwin and defined the city's requirements for habitability with more pronounced effect than any single individual or Northern Territory government policy. It rivals geology in its forcefulness, laying down conditions for where houses can be built (at least 1.5 kilometres back from known extensive and uncontrolled breeding swamps), how drains must work or roads be sloped, and where suburbs can be located. Darwin is on a peninsula, a ridge, hemmed in by Leanyer Swamp and Adelaide River on one side; by the harbour and mangroves with drainage problems on the other. Much of the higher land is reserved for Defence, including the airport. The trenches marking the no-man's land between housing and hazardous breeding grounds are marked by arterial roads, such as Vanderlin Drive, Tiger Brennan Drive and Elrundie Avenue in Palmerston. These roads do not direct civilians toward new grounds to occupy, but guard the borderlands that are not to be transgressed for urban living.

This has not stopped developers from insisting upon bad decisions. For newly-retired medical entomologist Peter Whelan, whose job for the last four decades has been to protect the people of Darwin from mosquito-borne diseases, the work of the entomology unit keeps expanding. As the population grows, so too does demand for land, and with it the press of humans into contact with mosquitoes, creating the perfect storm for such diseases as Ross River virus disease and Murray Valley encephalitis. Brackish marsh and mangrove areas, which flood only on the highest tide, present the greatest problems, and with more desirable land already occupied, these swamplands are increasingly made part of new urban neighbourhoods.

The most controversial development was Leanyer, a suburb developed at the insistence of the Commonwealth in the years when it was still directly administering Darwin. Leanyer sits adjacent to a brackish tidal reed swamp, a former municipal dump and, further afield, a practice bombing range. Compounding the area's unsuitability, new sewage ponds installed in 1974 blocked natural drainage from the mangroves, creating places where salt water from incoming tides could be trapped longer than four days, the critical timeframe for salt marsh mozzie larvae to mature into flying darts. A growing number of incoming drains from newly erected suburbs had turned the formerly seasonal swamp into a perennial one, with lush fresh water and brackish reeds: mosquito nirvana.

When the Commonwealth administration wanted a new suburb to build, Leanyer looked the easiest. Peter laughs at the feel of the words 'easy' and 'Leanyer' placed together in the one sentence, a wry chuckle which foretells the next forty years of hard yakka his team will face in rectifying the problems of trying to drain a dynamic, ever-evolving tidal swamp.

'They said, "Well, what if we just get rid of Leanyer Swamp?" I said, "Well, you can try. You can put in tide walls and you'll need a very exten-sive internal drainage system, but that probably won't be cheap.'"

The local objections were noted down, then meeting papers were jounced against the table and pens restored to pockets, clear signals to adjourn.

'They went away and got some advice and then came back and said, "We can drain it pretty easily. We'll just put a drain through the middle of it!"'

An engineer hired by Canberra administrators proposed the enticingly simple solution. If the gov-ernment put in one long, large drain across the floor of the swamp, from a drain outlet in the suburb of Malak out to the Leanyer sewage ponds, the swamp would not be a problem. Again, the entomologists warned that a single drain, with its poor drop to the ocean, would not be enough to empty the swamp. Again they were ignored. The drain was put in. It took some water out to sea but was too narrow to fully drain such an extensive area.

Mangrove forests are usually an entomologist's best friend. They facilitate drainage, encourage fish breeding and stabilise the silt. Provided there are no stagnant pits from poorly executed prop-erty developments or illegally dumped construc-tion rubble, mangroves alone do not indicate a mosquito problem. But when mangroves sink their tangled roots into the policy fantasy of a single drain, they will clog it up. And so the drainage system aimed at making Leanyer Swamp fit for suburban development became a new kind of pest for the cash-strapped entomologists. They had to become hydrological engineers, knowing that drains which sweep water out in one or two days are, by definition, also large enough to allow the tide to come back up, while anything slower than four days allows mosquitoes to breed. The delicate Goldilocks point of 'just right' — eventually reached through a network of lateral drains — had to be gleaned through trial and error and continual drain maintenance.

The draining system was one part of the challenge, but just outside of the Leanyer Swamp stands a bombing range used by military aircraft for practice runs. While the practice runs were finally stopped in the 1960s, the range is still full of unexploded ordnances. There were hundreds of bomb craters, in and beyond the target area, all on a salt flat. When the moon draws close to earth and pulls water up into the highest tides, the craters would fill with water and stagnate for weeks. Some species bred instantly, joined over the weeks by others, incubated by the generously filled wells.

'So that was a big project,' Peter says mildly, sipping his mug of coffee alternative. 'It was very hard for us to control. The concentration of insecticide has to be calculated on the depth of water, over hundreds and hundreds of hectares. Some areas you have shallow waters, other deep, some with unexploded ordnances lying in wait. We couldn't get the insecticide dosage accurate enough to kill the larvae in the deep craters without wasting a lot of money. Filling them in was the only option.'

With the help of the bomb-clearance unit and money from the Department of Defence, the expensive crater-filling project was a success. Yet residents and politicians still needed convincing that the dramatic suburban fogging programs they loved so much were less effective than dealing with known breeding and harbourage areas in off-sight swamps.

When Peter first started in the early 1970s — a new graduate from Adelaide University, but a born-and-bred Darwinite — the government practice was to fog some select urban areas during and soon after the wet season with DDT (changed to malathion in the mid-1970s). Old-timers fondly remember those foggers. Loudhailers would announce the vehicles slow-crawling down the streets, warning people to stay inside and shut their windows, but it was all too tempting to look out at the white mist being combed by striating yellow lights. The actress and pearling heiress Marilynne Paspaley remembers it with a typical nostalgia: 'It was an appealing sight – the blinking yellow lights of the truck with the machine pumping mist behind it. All the children of the neighbourhood used to skip behind it for a block or two. Who knew it was a mist of malathion?'

The foggers fell out of common use, but not because the poisons were ineffective. Far from it. DDT and malathion are magnificent chemical killers. Rather, Whelan's catch data showed that they were having little to no impact on mozzie reproduction or populations living in dense vege-tation, while killing many innocent critters in the process. The uselessness of fogging was a hard fact to put across to people. In the early years of mosquito control, there were few mechanisms for gathering baseline information on the insect's population densities across Darwin. Anecdote ruled. The team resorted to the human landing catch method – a technique where mosquitoes are counted as they come to feed on the human host. The target subjects would head out at dusk, sit near a suitable site, roll up their trousers and count everything that bit them in five minute intervals, using a rubber tube to suck the insect off their skin and blow it gently into a container. The work demanded patience, stamina and intense focus. It also made the gatherers vulnerable to disease: steel probes joined mozzie probes when annual blood tests were taken.

Today's methods for establishing population densities are less sacrificial, but just as resourceful. To get a sense of what the work of protecting the public involves, on a steamy morning in early January 2013 I visited the cluster of demountables on the grounds of Royal Darwin Hospital which hosts the Northern Territory's Entomology Unit of the Communicable Disease Control Branch. There are water eskies, boxes, Wellington boots and khaki shirts on pegs at the entrance, ready for the next field trips. It is almost homely, a scene from a log cabin porch in the Australian alpine country, only we are in the sultry tropical savanna, and the surrounding landscape is one of carparks, wire fences and hospital excavation works.

Every week and most days during the wet season, members of the entomology team head into the field to install or retrieve adult mosquito and ovitraps, and to sample for larvae in the swamps. The ovitrap is specially designed to detect such receptacle layers as the exotic dengue mosquito. It is a mesh-covered jam jar filled with water, made more delicious by a sprinkling of lucerne hay and oaten chaff. A skinny rectangular paddle, home-made from particle board with a wire hook at one end, is immersed in the jar. Eggs bind to the paddle, just as they might bind to a plant or other object as water retreats in the wild. Then it is a matter of removing the paddles back at the lab, drying them out, then rehydrating them, to see what hatches.

The ovitraps are placed at sentinel sites in and around Darwin and Palmerston. There are traps at the Robertson Barracks army base, in a plant nursery at Howard Springs, in a mechanic's driveway in Berrimah, behind someone's washing machine under a house in the northern suburbs, another where the fire brigade stores old bits of machinery and spare tyres. The spots chosen for jars are dark and out of the way, preferably near foliage, typical of Darwin conditions outside the city's mushrooming apartment blocks. Habitat-wise, mosquitoes remain in step with human developments. Different species will colonise vessels of fresh water in everyday places: a broken tennis ball, its inner socket facing the sky; a gardener's carefully stacked drip trays; a bird feeder. Team members drive from spot to spot, replacing old jars with new, recording data as they go, taking care not to get bitten.

Back at the entomology office, the paddles are incubated in a 3- by 4-metre 'ovitrap room'. For all its vials and samples, this small laboratory resembles the swamps in heat, smell and humidity levels. It is kept at a constant 35 degrees Celsius: the hotter and sweatier, the faster the mozzies breed and the quicker they grow. Larger hatchlings are extracted with a teat pipette and killed in an alcohol solution, twitching in protest as they die. This method preserves their bodies intact as it takes their breath away.

Does knowing the insects in such forensic detail make the entomology crew less fearful?

Hardly. The more they know, the more precautions they take. Mosquito-borne diseases are not nice to have. The arthritic pain years after contracting Ross River virus disease leads many sufferers to chronic depression. But entomological familiarity also breeds respect. Like jellyfish and crocodiles, the mosquito is a survivor, skilled in adjusting to new altitudes, temperatures and environments, developing immunity to insecticides and shifting its habits in relation to human actions, thus fully deserving a habitat in the place named after Charles Darwin. With global warming, they're poised to take advantage of the spread of salt marsh habitats as coasts are gradually inundated and new regions become warmer and wetter.

'What else is there to admire?' I ask.

'The colours. Some mosquitoes have the most vivid blues, or dramatic splashes of orange. Or a species might be separated by a single mark, ever so delicately defined, invisible to the naked eye. Each type is just so unique.'

Any reverence is tempered with practicality. The most surprising thing is how low-tech so many parts of the entomology operation are. Where money can be saved, it clearly is. Jam jars, homemade paddles, recycled plastic takeaway containers, hand-sewn sleeves. Even the laboratory shelving has been put up by staff labour. For these defenders of the human habitat, the technical paraphernalia can be both highly military, enabling a precise larvicide campaign, and very humble: a pen, a worksheet, a clipboard, a box of jars. And the work is mostly invisible. If asked to list the most critical infrastructure that is provided for them, it is unlikely the people of Darwin will register the work of the entomologists. Yet this front-line soldiering on a shoestring is as vital as the supply of power and water to making the town a place that can be lived in.

While mosquitoes might be fiercely democratic in their choice of human and ability to find new places to breed, their impact is nonetheless supremely differentiated. Mosquitoes both concentrate and highlight the contours of inequality. What the Australian Bureau of Statistics defines as low socioeconomic suburbs are joined at the hip to the best places for salt marsh mosquitoes and biting midges. These are suburbs where breezes are cut short and black mud releases sulphurous smells when the tides start receding. Suburbs adjacent to the troublesome Leanyer Swamps are also where public housing tenants, the poor, the newly migrated, the welfare-dependent are most densely located. In contrast, along the shoreline – where sea breezes blast mosquitoes away from blood targets – sits the elite suburb of Brinkin, occupied by professionals working at the nearby hospital and university or in the higher-paying tiers of the public service.

Yet in the case of Palmerston, a satellite town built 19 kilometres by road to the east of the Darwin peninsula, mosquitoes and entomologists have joined together in subverting the usual equations between affluence and amenity. Originally developed to supply affordable residential land for lower-income earners and welfare recipients, until recently it was known as 'Palmer-slum'. When it was being built, Darwin's swamps, storm-surge zones, flight path restrictions and Defence reserves precluded any further land releases in the immediate CBD. (Though now, One Mile Dam – an Aboriginal camp tucked away on scrub land granted over thirty years ago at the edges of the city – is eyed hungrily as a site for high-density accommodation. The push for housing is such that areas close to the city that were long avoided because of the biting insects have been developed. Bayview Haven, a marina development in former mangroves, goes by the tag Baygon Haven instead.)

In CBD terms, Palmerston is an outlier, reached by a long drive past industrial estates, big-box franchise stores and sandwich board signs advertising fruit trucks and massage services. Like the contact history of Australia, this dominant impression can be reversed. Driving into Darwin from the Stuart Highway positions Palmerston first.

Its land mass lightly slopes to mangrove forests fringing Darwin Harbour in the west and to the Elizabeth River in the south. It was a haven for biting insects, the mangrove biting midge in particular, a constant pest throughout the year. As the preferred site for housing commission estates, Palmerston's reputation suffered the usual fate of the poor: residents were blamed for everything, from dragging down real estate prices and standardised school test results to incubating juvenile crime gangs and paedophile rings. Yet, where Darwin's repeated failures to properly plan infrastructure for future needs have had to be rectified through protracted compromise, Palmerston was the first urban development in northern Australia to be co-planned with entomologists. To reduce insect bites to tolerable levels (calculated as no greater than one bite per minute), they advised a network of mown parklands and shady trees on one side of arterial roads and a buffer of privately owned rural blocks on the other, creating open windswept areas that separated suburbs from breeding grounds. Marlow Lagoon, a notorious mozzie site, was reconstructed into a deeper, less swampy body of water, while a program of dense tree planting replaced damaged scrub with shady, airy boulevards. With time, the suburbs emerged from the ravages of development all spacious and leafy, their schools large and green-lawned, not the asphalt playgrounds and red brick barracks people call schools down south. Natural drainage sites were formalised into channels and, best of all, Palmerston boasts the most advanced underground pipes and culverts: not too fat, not too thin, but just right.

So when it came to building extra housing for families of the Second Cavalry Regiment, it was Palmerston that became the preferred location, making it a key part of the most radical redirection of Australia's national defence strategy. And just as the stealthy *Aedes aegypti* is silent in her manoeuvres, Darwin's greater identity as a military town tends to be occluded from populist narratives of place. It helps make 'freedom' and 'lifestyle' the most frequently cited characteristics of this equatorial garrison town.

Chromaphobia

Gold! That brutal, elusive, malleable, beautiful, soft metal, older than money and more keenly desired. The ultimate fetish, it is what gives money its value. And when it was stumbled upon by men working the telegraph line in the Pine Creek region back in the 1870s, it turned the trickle of people seeking residency in the north into a flood of fortune seekers.

Once again, speculators on-sold to speculators: only a handful of diggings were actually worked with real muscle and machine. To solve the acute labour shortages, coolies were sought from Singapore and Hong Kong, Hakka and Punti alike. Many had been rendered homeless by the infamous Punti–Hakka clan wars in the Sze Yup counties of Guangdong, China, which escalated in scale and flame from 1855 on. Large numbers died, fled or were captured and on-sold as coolies, becoming part of a global Chinese diaspora, including the population of Australia's north. Hakka translates to 'guest' or visitor, while Punti (often also called Sze Yups, after their dialect) means 'original land'. To the white administrators, the Chinese were one; to the Chinese, they are many. The Chung Wah

Society divided its hall down the middle, Punti on one side, Hakka on the other, until Cyclone Tracy called a truce.

By February 1888 the Chinese outnumbered Europeans by a ratio of four to one, greatly unsettling the ever-anxious white administrators. Despite the alien landscapes they were brought into, the Chinese seemed to know how to make enterprises work. They are industrious. They don't stop working when the heat is at its most fierce, but retreat into shade to tend tools, re-knot fish nets, draw water from wells, cast seedlings from cuttings, make foods, sew, clean, sort their accounts. Only when it is late do they stop to play, releasing laughter and money with pai gow poker games and decorated mahjong tiles made into straights and groups.

They establish gardens, laundries, bakeries, dispensaries, restaurants and emporiums with goods sourced all the way from Hong Kong and beyond. They till and hoe, forcing market gardens to produce food using sinew and sweat. They work the docks and the railways and road gangs, and they form alliances to bid for new labouring jobs beyond those envisaged for them as coolies. It was their labour which built the few stone-crafted buildings that still remain of old Port Darwin, including the Government Residency and what is now known as Brown's Mart. Their work is reliable and costs one quarter of that of the white labourers.

It is an efficiency which brings them into direct competition with the ragtag of frontier men, who cannot help feeling the slight to their European heritage. Immersed in colonial sentiments, Chinese superiority presents a bit of a problem. They should not by rights or by ideology be better at anything but the disreputable and amoral. Resentments of the enclosed, disciplined worlds of the Chinese bred as fast as the poly-ethnic friendships. The White Australia Policy, with its notions of the 'yellow peril' at Australia's north, was one result.

Darwin was settled partly so that a relationship with northern neighbours could be had, and it has been hard to dislodge the idea that a white presence is needed to realise the trade advantages ostensibly conferred by facing the Timor Sea. It is one of the sustaining myths of settler colonialism, and it affects how history is told. As Regina Ganter puts it, Australian history should begin in the north, where it properly begins:

If we turn the map upside down and start
Australian history where its documentation
properly begins – in the north – the kaleidoscope
of Australian history falls into a completely
different pattern. Prior contact with Muslim
Asians on the north coasts and the cultural
bridge of the Torres Strait into coastal New
Guinea, make nonsense of the idea of an isolated
continent. Indeed, until World War II, whites were
heavily outnumbered in the north by close-knit
Asian and indigenous communities.

It is more conventional to begin with the voyages
of Captain Cook, take in settlement along the
country's south-east, track west and inland, before
eventually reaching the frontier north as the most
recent event. Yet, recast from a northern perspective, Australia gains a more elaborate, sophisticated
and older *recorded* history. For hundreds of years,
there was valuable trade with trepang collectors
and, with this, links with the European trading
empire that centred on the so-called Spice Islands
of the Indonesian and Malay archipelagos. The
port of Makassar was the centre of the trade, with
the uniquely repulsive-looking Australian trepang
attracting the very highest coin. Even today, only

a very few Darwinites in the non-Indigenous and non-Chinese population can trace their forebears back to the 19th century. And for all the accusations made against Aboriginal 'itinerants', the most transient group remains the European one.

Yet back when the Chinese were providing their indispensable labour and showing how the shackles of climate and geography could be unlocked, the white minority lost its nerve. A potentially successful model of multiculturalism was pulled apart before it could unravel the instinctive assumption of superior white governance. It was not for the Aborigines, the Chinese, the Japanese, the Malays or Filipinos to decide what kind of polity Darwin should have, that much was clear. Instead, the Northern Territory provided the catalyst for the White Australia Policy. Just as Darwin was starting to thrive, there was a growing fear that the Chinese would overrun the north, spill across borders and overwhelm the Australian colonies.

In 1881, the Territory's South Australian administrators showed their discontent with a special poll tax targeting Asian immigrants. In June 1888, as winter started to bite in Sydney, the colonial administrators convened the Intercolonial Conference on the Question of the Chinese, out of which came new legislation restricting the number of Chinese arriving on any vessel to one person per 500 tons of the ship's cargo. With administrators still not happy, the *Immigration Restriction Act* of 1901, aka the White Australia Policy, was put in place. A beautiful piece of colonial paranoia to mark the founding of Australian Federation, its final vestiges were only dismantled in 1973, under Gough Whitlam's brief reign. Until then, immigration officials could apply arbitrary dictation tests to those seeking to enter the country. More importantly for Chinese Darwinites at the time the Act was introduced, officials gained new powers of expulsion. Darwin's Chinese population shrank dramatically, making up only one quarter of the non-Indigenous population before the war in 1938.

The immigration policies wound their way into individual lives in intricate ways, long after and well beyond the original Chinese targets.

'It is why I married, to get divorced,' a long-time Darwinite told me. 'Can you imagine the pleasure when I got a divorce? Happy, happy, happy.'

A naturalised Australian, she was born in Italy, ending up in Darwin in search of true adventure. She was not a war refugee but a self-paying traveller, a fully independent woman. She pours me iced chinotto and calls me Teresa, my proper name, with such a sexy Italian emphasis it sounds anything but saintly.

'Those immigration officials then, they were like the SS, the Nazis. I knew who they were. I was not going to give them power over my life.'

She was talking about the time she needed to leave Darwin for Italy with her toddler, to seek a specialist's opinion about his weeping eyes. But first she made her de facto marriage official to ensure she could not be held to ransom by immigration officials with their ability to administer dictation tests in languages she might not know on her return. The divorce — something else she could pursue more safely with Whitlam's reforms — restored her treasured independence.

Darwin's Chinatown lasted until World War II. Today one can find a stalled attempt to resurrect this important architectural history, in a large excavated pit between Mitchell and Smith Streets, near the Birch, Carroll & Coyle cinema; and a 500-bay off-street car-parking complex, vertical Chinese lettering in gold against red running down a corner wall. The cement cubes of the Chinatown car park are a far cry from what came before. The smell in Darwin's old Chinatown was of woodsmoke, spices, raw meat, barely alive fish writhing in shallow pails of water, dried seafood, chicken poop and wilting compost. Shrines wafted the scent of joss sticks, the beckoning smoke meeting the ancestors who, cold in the celestial heavens, would come closer to the welcome warmth, coaxed into better hearing distance of the wishes of the living. Wiry men and women, clavicle bones indented from the weight of the carrying pole, would patter past with retooled kerosene tins heavy with newly made bricks, wood, fruit, rice. Others might occasionally idle in the shade of shop awnings, using tree stumps as stools, stained fingers delivering tobacco smoke to lungs.

The semi-orderly shopfronts of old Chinatown gave way at their rear to mud lanes and flimsy structures elevated over drains, patched together with mud-filled rice sacks and paperbark poles, strips of corrugated iron, bits and pieces of canvas and cloth. A strong wind could tumble them down. In 1897, a strong wind does — one of the three cyclones that has pulled Darwin to its knees since

Goyder first mapped the town for its absent investors. The buildings were renewed and replaced, until World War II, when the Commonwealth assumed all landholdings and directed Darwin's redevelopment through the usual strategies of bold talk, centralised planning and underinvestment.

For visitors like Elsie Masson, adventuring in Darwin for a year as *au pair* for the Administrator John Gilruth and his family, Chinatown was the liveliest part of town. As Masson described it, a newcomer in 1912

> sees people of every colour, until she feels she is turning the leaves of a book of patterns ranging from the deepest chocolate to pale cream. Black Aborigines throw spears on open grassed spaces between the houses; dusky Malays, short and sturdy, sit smoking by the railway; children of all shades of brown peer with curious eyes round the tin walls of their homes; yellow, wrinkled Chinese, in blue silk trousers, carrying baskets slung on poles, pass at a shuffling trot.

The Chinese tenements also drew local residents, who, like Darwinites today, loved and loathed their ethnically diverse town. For the ruling gentry, the ones who invested most heavily in the symbols of social distinction, Chinatown was a diversion from their slower-moving worlds. Then they would retreat to the quiet of shaded verandahs to bemoan the unsanitary conditions and the vices of the Chinese. In the newspapers, the Chinese were accused of running prostitution rackets even as the finger-pointers might steal down the alleyways late at night for a pipe of opium, bets on the cockfighting, or a touch of 'black velvet': Aboriginal women, socially reviled and just as intensely desired.

The guilty white pleasures from the town and its hinterland soon created a problem for the uptown governors: too many Chinese and too many 'yeller-fellers'. And then there was the vexed problem of how to make the Indigenous population amenable to the plantation-style indentured labour Anglo colonists need for successful equatorial living. Without domestics, a Commonwealth inquiry of 1936 into northern industries would note, Anglo women suffered all the disadvantages of the tropics and none of the 'usual compensations which tropical countries provide, such as hours of leisure, social intercourse and labour for household duties'. Compounds were built to keep the hybrid Aboriginal population from running freely through the streets in full public glare, and to make inmates available for the dreary business of maintaining settlers in the manner to which they would like to be accustomed.

For Aborigines, it is a time of curfews and righteous religious instruction, the berated audience forced to swallow the contradictions of good Christian settlement. The authorities gave reasons for European men to fear marrying Aboriginal women and backed them with legislation. Social judgements did the work of policing too. Swift ostracism of the explicit sinner, the 'combo', was harsh and instinctive. The good ladies and gentlemen of Darwin deplored with a moral rectitude that stiffened their spines and tightened their lips. Their aversion was as readymade as my own prissiness when I spot a red-hued Aussie male draping his blancmange arms over a young Asian girl. It is a compulsive judgement that needs no intimate knowledge of circumstances.

While words were not always needed, in case words were required the Protectors of Aborigines have documented powers to control money, movement, mateship. They make registers of Aboriginal births, known far and wide as 'the stud book', to indict, divide, permit and govern. The lighter the children's skin, the more intimately they are dragged into the vortex of racist, benevolent, violent, capricious, loving, controlling white households.

And yet, life in the tropical frontier was also lived in the breach, between the rules and their thwarting, the barriers and their crossings. And so, despite the compounds and the rules, the judgements, fines and jailings, the population retained its hybrid layers. White men who wanted to marry Aboriginal women were embraced in the ostensible margins even as they were dealt a social shudder from the sanctified centre. 'There were class distinctions within each nationality as well as racial distinctions that impacted the whole community,' wrote Susan Sickert in her account of Asian–Aboriginal–European interrelations in the tropical town of Broome, Darwin's westerly cousin. She could have been describing the inner workings of the northern capital. It is a hierarchy in which Aboriginal people were placed at the bottom, outcasts in their own land. Then came the coolies, the indentured Asians who were brought in for the endless drudge work of colonial settlement. They mixed with the mixed race people and other piece-rate labourers, the lumpenproletariat, the groups who, in Xavier Herbert's hands, live life at a drunken edge in the strange back parts of the town, in places like Police Paddock, where Stuart Park now is, or the dockyards.

Between these and the minority Europeans came the Asian merchants and property owners, 'some of the mixed race population who had citizenship rights or, in the case of women, had married foreign men'. As Lieutenant Colonel R.H. Weddell (a former Administrator whose name is soon to be memorialised as Darwin's latest satellite town, Weddell) later complained to the Commonwealth, a grave problem of 'half-caste coloured aliens' had been breeding in North Australia, 'owing to the unrestricted intermarriage of alien coloured races with aboriginals and half-castes, the result of which has been the accumulation of a hybrid coloured population of a very low order'. These dangerous hybrids, he warned, 'constitute a perennial, economic and social problem and their multiplication throughout the north of the continent is likely to be attended by grave consequences to Australia as a nation'.

Not all Darwin's Chinese lived in the shanties. After the rebuild, some built houses where they could catch a sea breeze and access the shoreline, dragging nets and tending traps laced with bits of pork to lure snapping crabs out from the mud and into the wok. Life wasn't easy for the Chinese, even if they knew how to be self-sufficient, fourth-generation Darwinite Laurence Ah Toy reminds me. His father Jimmy and his mother Lily Ah Toy were renowned pioneers of industry at Pine Creek, where their store still operates, from the time of the mines to today. 'We could never understand why my mother Lily cherished boiled eggs so much,' son Laurence recalls – until they learnt that those eggs were currency, produced by the family's hens, but sold to others. There was only one special day when Lily received an egg of her own to eat: her birthday.

There is much written about Lily Ah Toy in the annals of Darwin. She was kind to oral historians and generous with her memorabilia. Her story in the archives is full of homely detail, telling of the drudgery of watering their market garden with pails hand-drawn from their well; the heat of their stringybark house with its bits of galvanised roofing and dirt floor; the special cakes made in the ant-bed oven; the elaborate preparations for Chinese New Year and other festivals. Rice was thrown for the roosters at her wedding, to distract them from visiting the celebration with malevolent spirits. Lily hints too of the clandestine domain of the Chinese community, the way families preferred their own counsel and networked together, keeping the whites at arm's length from their familial worlds. Her account of Chinese insularity sparks the curiosity of her first interviewer, the historian Ann McGrath.

'Did you ever visit white households?' Ann asks.

'No, you – they got to invite you before you visit them and they never ask me to go along. It didn't worry me because I am not used to doing that,' Lily replies. And later, after she marries Jimmy Ah Toy and moves to Pine Creek, Ann probes further: does Lily ever go to the races, or the rodeo? Are there special picnic days, perhaps?

No again. 'I don't remember going to any of them. There could be, but then of course I didn't take part in it … we still old-fashioned Chinese, you keep yourself to yourself.'

The white settlers would write about the imperturbable, wily Chinaman, but the Chinese left fewer public records of their thoughts, while the non-writing Aboriginal groups had their memories recorded only patchily. 'Life in Darwin' – wrote Elsie Masson – 'is made up of many little worlds, each continuing in its own way, impinging on but never mingling with the others'.

True, but as we know, heat melted barriers too, and relationship tendrils between European, Asian and Aboriginal townsfolk were wending into these separate worlds from the outset. Darwin's proudly poly-ethnic community depends on no less. As a girl, Lily Ah Toy and her family were living at the top of Gardens Hill golf course, growing crops that were raided by the starving kids from Kahlin Compound, where 'coloured' children, and sometimes their mothers, were jailed under the all-embracing and flexible miscegenation laws. For the underfed children from Kahlin, hunger would overcome their fear of the sharp-talking Chinese who might hunt them out, shaking spikes and shovels in warning.

Val McGinness was one of the hungry Kahlin boys who snuck down to the Chinese plots, drawn by a 'beautiful paddock of sugar cane'. He squeezed through the wire strands to where Chinamen were hoeing their vegetables, choosing a juicy, fat stalk for his target. But his knife was so blunt 'you could have rode on it'. He hacked and hacked, then bent the stalk apart, making such a loud popping noise the gardener was fully alerted. Val bolted into a lawn of sleepy weed and his mates beyond the fence fled back over the flat, leaving him for dead.

'I don't know how the Chinaman never saw me because here was this beautiful lawn and right in the middle of it was this big lump ... and that was me under there!'

After sweating and crying for what seemed like hours, convinced he would be shot at any moment, Val bolted under cover of darkness back up the hill to the Compound.

It's the trouble with these histories. I can guess the gardener knew Val was in there but not what the Chinese thought about the children locked in the huts up on the hill. When I talk to old Dar-winites, they remember a simple racial harmony, not like the troubles of today, they will add. Too much welfare, people nod, circulating the current policy indictment as if it is fully self-explaining.

The transition from feared yellow hordes to

valuable members of the community has been remarkable. Lily was the daughter of Darwin-born Moo Linoy, in turn the son of patriarch Moo Yat Fah. My children's surname is also 'Moo'. It is an Anglicisation of a Hakka name, bestowed (in my mind's eye) in an unimaginative gesture of colonial officialdom back in 1881, when Moo Yat Fah first came to Darwin, bringing his skills as a carpenter to repair work on the Resident's House and the Darwin–Pine Creek railway. He had left his wife and their firstborn son, Moo Tam Bing, nicknamed Pompey, back in Hong Kong until he felt secure enough to bring them over. Pompey is Moo Linoy's older brother, and my children's great-grandfather. The Moo family still look to that Gardens Hill site that Lily describes – long lost to the compulsory acquisitions of wartime Darwin – as their original estate. I guess the local Larrakia do the same.

Members of the Hakka diaspora, especially the second wave immigrants from Timor, now own significant businesses, such as the shopping complex Jape Homemaker Village. The Ah Toys are respected policy advisers and statesmen, while Dr Ken Moo took advice from the doctor and Catholic priest Reverend Frank Flynn and became a widely respected ophthalmologist. The Punti can claim the first Chinese mayor in Darwin, Harry Chan, a man who was said to have known the names of almost all Darwin's residents and those of their domestic pets. Chan was followed by the country's first Australian-born Chinese (ABC) Lord Mayor, the Punti Alec Fong Lim, whose legacy as Darwin's eleventh Lord mayor has been continued into the present, with his daughter Katrina Fong Lim wearing the mayoral robes today.

Meantime, members of the Chung Wah Society's Dragon and Lion Dancing Troupe have a different battle on their hand: managing their raging popularity. In the fortnight of Chinese New Year celebrations, the troupes perform over 300 blessings. Speaking to the coordinators in March, I learn their dance calendar is already full for the year, a surge in demand that is led by non-Chinese people. School assemblies, birthdays, corporate functions, sponsored events, community festivals, even a Buddhist temple need to be blessed. The evening I watched them, it was May, and they had been called upon to bless the opening of the 2013 season of the Mindil Beach Markets, together with a vacant plot of land someone intends to develop in the future.

A pride of five lions performed that evening, moving their way through dense crowds of people pushing prams, cradling mango smoothies or eating chicken wings that oozed a fatty aroma into the evening heat. The lions ducked and darted through the throng, their path broadcast by young women in black karate pants and yellow T-shirts with red banding, clashing cymbals and vigorously beating drums. The dancers are all volunteers, young men in the main, as menstrual blood intercepts the forces of good luck. Yet it is the female musicians who dictate the dancer's moves. They drove the lions past the massage tents and craft stalls, the didgeridoo sellers and ice-cream stands. A lion would stop at a stall, duck, leap up and jag its giant head dramatically from one side to the other, snapping its jaws and widening its bobbling eyes with each staggered pause. Children screamed, tucking their heads into their mothers' skirts, turning back quickly, greedy for the thrill of safe terror.

As joyously friendly as the lions seem, as they occasionally nuzzle each other before returning to the job at hand – to bring prosperity – they must ward away evil spirits with even greater fearsomeness. This takes aggressive determination. Physical stretching, stern exercise, diet, sleep. It is a regime that seemingly might keep young people away from being dancers. It does the opposite. Children can join as baby lions, a recently introduced gradation system to handle growing youth interest in becoming a troupe member. The system also helps to meet mounting public demand by training dancers and musicians across the full repertoire, from the blessings used for religious observances through to forms of street dance.

I wanted to learn about lion and dragon choreography and, especially, what Darwin looks like from a dancer's perspective. I had learnt from my old schoolmate Gavin Chin that dancer turnover is high, as the young people reach the end of high school and head 'down south' for university, then get too busy establishing families and professions to return to the troupe. Curious, I watched a dance training session one Saturday afternoon at the Chung Wah Society Hall. 'Hot is what it is,' said one dancer, to the nodding grins of others. He could have added 'and exacting'. There are a finite number of ways in which a lion dancer playing the head should execute a forward punch or kick, to land both head and tail in a stance ready for the next fast-paced move. They learn control so that they might loosen the rules, to exhibit free lion spirit through impromptu nuzzles and paw play. Rigour and infinite variation also guide the serpentine movements of the longer dragon. At least nine dancers coordinate the fierce, yet wise and compassionate, moves of this magical creature. Theirs is a restricted field of tassels and cloth folds, bent backs, sweat, panted communication, anticipated choreography, the clack of bamboo poles and the constant urging of drums and cymbals. Once, the heads were made of fibreglass and weighed a ton. Now they are made of papier-mâché and can be elevated to new heights, but still, the dancers can only see the world in glimpses and snatches.

For the perfect blend of discipline and flamboyance, the dancers must practice via the deceptive fluidity of martial arts training. One exercise had the dancers standing in a circle, holding chairs aloft in front of their chests, arms stretched horizontally, legs apart, knees bent, while they count out a beat, each dancer shouting the next number in sequence, starting at one. By the time 'Two hundred and forty' is grated out, feet are skidding outward, smaller children have to rest their chair, older athletes are grimacing. Arms and legs quiver, sweat stings eyes and stains clothes. Finally, at 300, the coach relents: they can put the chairs down.

Exhausted from watching their relentless physicality, I walked out of the training session into the blazing midafternoon light, down Cavenagh Street to 'the new Woolies'. The streets were near empty – Darwin is not a town for idle pedestrians, at least not before dusk on a hot weekend afternoon. I remember squinting up at yellow and navy long-sleeved cotton shirts, the tradie's signature uniform, as they flapped against verandah railings on high-rise apartment buildings, where tiny metal porticos provided scant shade against the blasting tropical sun. Does this town disappoint those tourists who make the mistake of walking in the city, in forlorn search of the Darwin they've heard is the most Asian of Australia's capital cities? Amid the great secular ugliness of the CBD they would find a car park instead of a Chinatown, for Darwin's multiculturalism is not well packaged. Yet the lack of ethnic enclaves somehow seems fitting. Darwin's poly-ethnic make-up is such a naturalised part of everyday life, it has no need to fabricate special districts or ornamental displays. It's embodied in the intergenerational sweat that keeps Chinese traditions alive within the general community; in the

Aboriginal families bearing diasporic surnames; in the memories of families divided and torn, yet resilient and surviving; and in the troubles of an Italian woman returning to a place whose blurring of racial divides both invoked and made a joke of the White Australia Policy. Perhaps Chinese lettering decorating a cement carpark, that most mundane yet functional of architectural forms, is an apt representation after all.

Levelling the field

It was a solid piece of mining waste, heavy as an empty dumpster, that crashed into their smoko that hot November Friday in 1918. Brothers Jack and Bernard McGinness, their brother-in-law Harry Edwards and 'Tommy the blackboy' had been working the Lucy Tin Mine on the Darwin River when the hefty piece of mullock broke away from the hanging wall. Harry was the luckier one, bursting through the debris out to where his brother-in-law Jack was standing. Young Bernard McGinness was knocked unconscious, trapped beneath a thick lump. The task almost overwhelmed the three men — Jack, Harry and Tommy too, doing his best through the pain of his own wound. Heave as they might, they could not lift the weight from Bernard's trapped body. One plied a pick, while the two others shifted the debris. Finally, Bernard was freed enough for Harry to splash water over him, sufficient to pull him back to consciousness but not powerful enough to mend his sprained ankle or the painful wounds wracking his side. These would take time to heal, though no bones had been broken.

You could say 1918 was a tough year for the McGinness family. This was the year of the Darwin Rebellion, when locals menaced Administrator Gilruth so thoroughly he fled his post. It was the year the Commonwealth tightened the regulatory screws of earlier Aboriginal Ordinances with a new term, 'quadroon', to further subdivide the town's mulatto population. Two months before the 1918 accident, their father Stephen had died. The poison from an untended leg wound had crept through his blood and stolen his life.

Stephen's death changed everything. It both tore the family apart and pulled them together. It triggered a chain of events that would, in time, help create the 1967 referendum on the alteration of the Australian Constitution. After the referendum, the Commonwealth could make special laws for 'aboriginal natives' as it already could for 'the people of any race' and the whole of section 127 was removed. Section 127 had made the massive world transitions affecting Aboriginal populations literally measureless: 'In reckoning the numbers of the people of the Commonwealth, or of a State or other part of the Commonwealth, aboriginal natives should not be counted,' it had decreed, until Australians voted otherwise.

When Aboriginal people finally counted, their unmistakable ascendancy in football shone through. To be clear: by 'football' we mean Aussie Rules, a game the north did not invent but has made its own. Of all the states and territories, the Northern Territory has the highest percentage of its population participating in Australian football. Indigenous players from the north complete the elite teams in the south; AFL incentive schemes entice students to stick with school; whole music, art and craft festivals are built around the game.

As it's played in Darwin, it is a hard, hot game. The season starts in the build-up, before the monsoon breaks, when the air is so saturated with moisture, the body's own secretions give no relief at all. Under the football guernsey, the body glows. Tiny beads of sweat form miniature bubble-wraps on the forehead, above the lip, below the eyelashes, on the sternum, between legs and toes. A small home game advantage comes with knowing where the ginger ant nests are and shepherding opponents to their telltale gritty mounds, for any player will lose concentration slapping off the tormenting swarms. But everyone sweats, heat remaining the great equaliser. The game rewards agility, sprightliness, accuracy, the ability to catch a ball on the tip of a finger. It's the guy who scrambles up the back of another, arms outstretched, snatching the ball out of air; the player who spins the ball end over end, high and long, the crowd's breath held … it's there.

Today, football is celebrated as the greatest of social levellers. Think of footie and the multiethnic names of the great Darwin extended families come to the fore – Cubillo, Motlop, McGinness, Hazelbane, Ah Mat, Bonson, Lew Fatt, Raymond, Angeles, Rioli, MacLean. The seemingly easy multiculturalism of the football team is how people prefer to remember 'old' Darwin, the Darwin where everyone knew everyone and there were no colour politics. Funny, then, to consider it was colour politics that gave Darwin its beloved code in the first place.

The Irishman Stephen McGinness had married Alyandabu, also known as Lucy, some time around 1900. The date is not exact but the love binding them was true. They had five children: four boys, Barney, Jack, Joe and Val, and one bonny girl, sister Margaret. Steve was a cheerful drinker, known for 'his occasional weekend visits to Darwin when many a merry hour was spent at the Victoria Hotel' and a hard worker. He had been a ganger on the northern railway until he'd lost his job after an accident killed a man in his charge. The family opted to leave Darwin in search of work, heading to Bynoe Harbour further along the coast. Mother Lucy was relieved. They were getting out alive — that was all that really mattered. As one of the few survivors of her people, the Kungarakan language group, Alyandabu knew all too well how often Aboriginal families veered closer to death than life when found in the wrong place at the wrong time.

It was Alyandabu who spotted a weathered lump of what turned out to be tin, south-west of Darwin. When Stephen went to register the claim in 1908, it was only right that it be made out in Alyandabu's name. He called it the Lucy Tin Mine, using her European name to disguise their political statement. Working the mine was hard, but during downtimes they would camp, taking their milking goats as they roved, filling the children's heads with tales of evil spirits and Dreaming infractions mixed in with Irish hobgoblins, wailing ghosts and Catholic pieties. No one danced an Irish jig better than Alyandabu. Stephen's death changed everything, but so did his love for Alyandabu.

Let us pull away from the tin mine and the ten years of happiness before 1918, past Alyandabu's survival of the Kungarakan killings, back to an even earlier time. Back to an event that had nothing to do with the Kungarakan and yet swept them up too, in the killing fields of South Australian rule. Let's wind back to 3 September 1884, and pan further to the west of Darwin, to a copper mine over on the Daly River. This was the day three white males working a shaft there were mortally speared and a fourth was fearfully injured. To the families living in the region, the men were known rapists. To the enraged white citizens, it was black treachery, demanding many reprisals, swift and fierce, too many to count. South Australian financiers provided the means, the government provided the armoury, police organised the leaders, riled volunteers rounded out the numbers. White outrage still gripped six years after the event, as the newspaper reminded its readers of the terrible events:

> A band of aboriginals attacked and foully
> murdered Landers, Noltenuius and Schollert
> and at the same time left Harry Roberts, the
> only survivor, for dead along with the rest ...
> Previously they had found the natives useful
> without signs of treachery and on the day of
> the massacre they had gone to work unarmed
> and thoughtless of danger. While three of the
> prospectors were engaged in a shaft and Schollert
> was working the kitchen a few yards off, the blacks
> pounced on them and in a space of time briefer
> than it takes to tell it here, they had inflicted
> injuries upon the helpless white men from the
> effects of which only one survived, and only in
> that instance because of his being fearfully hurt
> and apparently lifeless.

The South Australian Minister for Justice and

for the Northern Territory authorised four private raiding parties to avenge the deaths of the three copper miners. A separate police party set out under the sharpshooter Corporal George Montagu, fresh from his previous appointment as 'Inspector of Slaughter Houses and of Brands and Skins'. The posses fanned out, shooting families from Daly River in the west all the way to present-day Kakadu National Park in the east, as relentless as the Japanese bombings and as under-reported. No warrants were needed, only a judicious haziness as to who was an offender and the number of deaths required to exact retribution. The killings went on for over a year. Who can say what proportion of people died when a people do not count enough to be counted?

Montagu's report, like all good public service evaluations, shared his important learnings:

What other parties have done I do not know but I believe the natives have received such a lesson this time as will exercise a salutary effect over the survivors in the time to come. One result of this expedition has been to convince me of the superiority of the Martini-Henry rifle, both for accuracy of aim and quickness of action.

The Martini-Henry, an army-issue gun favoured throughout the British Empire for its deadly force, used bullets so heavy that, fired at a range under 200 yards (180 metres), a round could pass through one body and hit another standing behind. Those rifles did the job of bulldozers in clearing the land for cattle and, later, for Australia's vast ripping, shipping and military activities.

Advice on the government-sanctioned Martini-Henry did not discourage killings by other means. Family members from the Kungarakan people, displaced custodians of the paperbark lands between the Finnis and Darwin Rivers, had gathered at a camp at the Stapleton railway siding, some 50 kilometres south of Darwin. Food was always scarce, now that hunting was so hard and the land choked with the foul sweat of hard men with guns and other weapons: tobacco, white flour and grog. So when poisoned damper was handed out, its baking powder laced with weed killer, people ate eagerly to fill hungry bellies.

'The majority of the tribe ... about one hundred people, became victims of poisoned damper,' son Joe McGinness would later write in his autobiography. 'Those who ate the poisoned damper became violently ill before their death.'

Despite seeing her families murdered, Alyandabu did not have it in her heart to hate white people. Instead, she married the handsome Irish immigrant Stephen, and they worked the mine for ten years from 1908 to 1918, raising children and goats. Their daughter Margaret married Harry Edwards, a 'blacksmith and boring contractor', whose skills were handy too. But then, in October 1918, Stephen died, and everything changed. Despite being a registered part-owner, Alyandabu's claim was forfeited and Aboriginal protection authorities insisted their two youngest children, Valentine and Joseph, now officially classified as fatherless half-castes, be taken to Kahlin Compound.

Alyandabu chose to join them there, forcing her slight figure from one physically demanding job to another, to be near her boys. She would sneak them leftovers from the table of one Judge Waters, in whose home she worked as laundress and housemaid, 'as we got very little or sometimes nothing to eat during the day'. Joe was only five years old when he was compounded and food was often on his mind. His older brother Val could risk the wrath of Kahlin superintendent Bob MacDonald, 'a tyrant of the first order', to raid the neighbouring Chinese gardens, but young Joe learnt his own tricks. He'd watch Val join the slick of sweaty shoulders on the barely grassed Kahlin football fields and learnt some key moves, the kind you can't get out of books. There were all sorts of strategies played out on the field: tactics for surprising your opponents, ways to settle differences with actions and few words, the need to conciliate. When Joe later became the first Aboriginal president of the Federal Council for Aboriginal Advancement in 1961, after serving in Borneo during World War II and learning the ropes as a wharfie and active member of the Waterside Workers Federation, he'd put those skills to use.

Kahlin oval was a buffer from the small, hot, weatherboard huts of the Compound, replacing its micro-surveillances and petty governance with the adventure and manly respect of hard, hot games. Yet it also reproduced the town's social distinctions, for no boys from Kahlin were meant to play beyond Compound grounds. Football clubs proper were for properly white men. The season starts in the build-up because of the primacy accorded to that other great colonial game, cricket. For cricket to be played in the dry, when the grounds don't swallow the little red ball, footy was shifted to the wet.

Built in 1913, where the elite suburb of Larrakeyah now blends into the new marina full of trophy houses known as Cullen Bay, Kahlin Compound was a devilish hard place, 'a miniature city of whitewashed hovels crowded on a barren hill above the sea', where even the hospital 'looked something like the latrines of a military camp'. This concentration camp for coloureds was the brainchild of Baldwin Spencer, who had not imagined it as a place of cruel incarceration but of systematic improvement. Then as now, the reformist idea among interveners focused on the magical power of disciplined labour to yield psychic transformation. But as is so often the case with schemes for northern social developments (less Ponzi than preposterous), the mean finances and pathetic expertise invested into the promising reformist vision made Kahlin a place of starvation rations, closed-in walls and strict rules and curfews. The unofficial lessons taken up by the families were something else again. There is a Darwin fellowship that, forged out of shared indignities, is marked by its humour, resilience and creativity. It is the comradeship of taking care of your friends and family within a field of arbitrary adversity.

The vision behind the incarceration was morally upright enough. Protected from the worst depravities of the wild white men and savage myalls at loose on the frontier within the safety of compounds, half-castes and quadroons would find a more useful social slot. They might even provide a model for their darker brothers and sisters out bush. Learning to work as lower-order domestics, gardeners, rock diggers and builders, the children and babies from mixed couplings would learn the value of devoting their time to a new social order, one where labour is not directed at asking the land for its productivity in kind, but at producing different kinds of ends (a delight in dust-free writing bureaus, for example) for different kinds of means — not songlines, but partially paid or withheld wages.

True enough, there were powerful learnings to be had from this reefing of people away from relations with the cosmos and toward time-clock dedication, then making them beg for paltry earnings. As Val McGinness tells in his oral history recording:

So this day, look I was really mad at this system that they had. And I went up to them and [the official, Mr Partridge, said]: 'Yes, Val. How much money do you want?'

'Oh,' I said, 'I'd like to have five pounds please, Mr Partridge' – that was big money, you know, five pounds.

'What? Five pounds, is it? What are you going to do with five pounds?'

It had absolutely nothing to do with him, you see. I said: 'Oh, I've got to pay for my lessons, Mr Partridge.'

'Lessons? What sort of lessons are you taking?'

I said: 'I'm learning to mind my own business, Mr Partridge.'

Men like Val bounced frontier reasoning on its head and spun it in a new direction, foreshadowing the skilled football players and activists they would become. They played because playing was not the same as working for the man. It was thrilling. Courageous. Elegant and beautiful in ways that toughened Territory boys could accept. It meted out hard-won respect. And it was deeply political.

'Oh, we played football,' recalled Val McGinness, 'but football those days was different football to what it is now … We played with a vengeance because it was the black man against the white man. It was war when we got on the field.' The sun burnt their backs, the sweat made the leather ball even more slippery, but on and off field, footie was the training ground for more rebellious forms of organisation, including fierce unionism, a growing ability to articulate dissent and, for the women, a burning desire not to have to ask nicely to do something as simple as go out for a walk.

One Wednesday in March 2013 I met up with Geoffrey Angeles, or 'Jacko' as he is locally known, a former Darwin Buffaloes player and direct McGuinness descendant (there is some dispute about when the 'u' appears in the surname). 'Hey you,' we had greeted each other, Darwin-style, as the last of Sydney's summer heat cocooned the

southern city ahead of cooler autumn winds. Jacko
was at the University of Sydney to support Indigenous medical students and to talk more widely to
hundreds of undergraduates on Indigenous health:
an immense, unresolved, life-and-death subject he
had to compress into digestible lecture portions.
The Sunday prior, I had been running a gauntlet
of trolley-pushers in a crowded Sydney shopping centre when Jacko had caught my surprised
attention. To my homesick eye he was clearly a
Darwin man, tall, broken-nosed, with the easy
lope of an Aussie rules football player, immediately discernible. Not stick-thin, pale and artfully
coiffed, inner-Sydney style, but broad-shouldered
and long-sighted, a man used to scanning hori-
zons for signs and sounds. 'Hey you' had burst
out of me then as well. He returned the greeting
with an upward thrust of his chin and broad smile,
nodding with patient good humour while I bab-
bled about the good fortune of meeting him of
all people, in this of all places, given my current
obsession with all things Darwin.

We agreed to meet on campus to talk about
fishing, football and life in Darwin – good topics
for a man whose recipes for crispy whiting, numus
and pearl meat salad featured in the first season

of *Poh's Kitchen*, the ABC television show hosted by artist and runner-up Australian MasterChef Poh Ling Yeow. Jacko's numus requires freshly caught, firm-fleshed white fish, lemons or limes, vinegar, chilli, delicate pinches of this and that – magic ingredients that will take the pickled fish to its point of perfection with a cold beer.

Jacko is the grandson of Jack McGinness, whose campaigns for Indigenous rights with his brothers Barney, Val, Joe and sister Maggie culminated in the 1967 referendum. The family garnered public support for the votes that would help make Indigenous people be counted. Our talk roves over the great political battles waged since the 1930s, the importance of taking people for who they are and the fine art of making fish traps. Government regulations had deemed the fish traps, made to traditional methods, illegal; decades of political agitation later, the regulations were overturned.

'Commercial fishing can rape vast kilometres of sea country and kill unwanted sea creatures by the ton; but the stand-alone fish trap which never moves, where we just take what we need for a feed and return the rest – uninjured – to sea, well, that's not allowed!' Jacko says, exasperation furrowing his words.

Footie weaves in and out of the tale, as if the story itself is the elliptical ball, darting and dodging en route to the posts before time runs out and lessons with the medical students resume. Like his cousins, friends and elders before him, football had taken Jacko to other places, to matches interstate and to southern cities. It was these exposures that highlighted the ethical world kids from Darwin had made, on and off the field.

'Without us knowing it, us people from Darwin were practising multiculturalism before that word even got into the dictionary,' he says.

'You know, I can remember going down south for football and it was the first time we got called "black bastards". It was a shock. We were called names back home but they weren't colour-coded like that. No one got called race terms in Darwin, white or black. I remember one time when an Aboriginal spectator who probably wasn't from Darwin insulted a footie player by calling him a "white C-word". And one of our mob decked him. Gave him a good hit to educate him that us mob up here don't say those kind of things to white people. And white people knew the same lesson – they don't say those things to us. Those terms cut deep.

'It's not as if we didn't experience racism. But we never took that separatist path. We defeated racists by not becoming them.

'It's like how Grandpa Jack McGinness said it, when the Chief Protector asked him "What is it that you really want?", inferring he was a whinger or something, you know? Grandpa Jack eloquently replied, "I am glad you asked that question. Because all I ever want is to enjoy the company of my fellow man — black, white or brindle."

'It's like that. We just fought our politics through wit and humour, and the mix of different cultural groups playing together in the Buffaloes Club.

'You seen that documentary, *Buffalo Legends*, that Paul Roberts and Kootji Raymond made?' Jacko asks, parrying my questions about Darwin, race and football with one of his own.

I hadn't but soon do. 'The Legends', many of them Kahlin boys, were the foundation players of the Buffaloes Football Club, a team the Moo family also played for, my husband and his brothers and their uncles before them. The re-enacted documentary narrated by Bill Dempsey, himself a footie legend, shows how Buffs emerged as the club for Darwin's coloured community. This was the club for Darwin's Chinese, Aborigines, Greeks, Filipinos and even 'nigger-loving' white people. It was for anyone not able or wanting to pass as pure Anglo to play and plot as they pushed against the town's segregation policies. To raise club money in defiance of fundraising bans, the men formed gambling rings, playing a Chinese game of poker, pai gow, with youngsters on the lookout for police. In the film, Jacko plays a dual role: one as a coach for the early legends; one as young Val as he takes on the overseer in asking for his own wages. Jacko's a suave figure in dance scenes too, showing the Sunshine Club where Stuart Park and Parap families swayed to jazz and slow swing. Contemporary families gather to yarn, easily breaking into shared song and hearty laughter, an allusion to the many singers and songwriters these football families can boast. The film finishes as only a film about Darwin footie can, with footage of Robbie Ah Mat (later scooped up by Collingwood) taking on the opposition with his electrifying speed, gliding the ball upfield before kicking a long, beautiful shot.

Playing football mingled affinities and antagonisms, on and off the field. Darwin's silvertails, those men who dressed in white jackets and lounged on shaded verandahs, their brows furrowed with the worries of colonial administration, had started their own club, the Waratahs, exclusively for Anglos. The town's coloured fringes wanted a club of their own. First registered as the Warriors, then as Vesteys (after the meat factory where some of the players were employed), it became the Darwin Buffaloes, champion club for Darwin's underdogs. Jacko's grandfathers, Jack McGinness and Tim Angeles, fought political battles and played for the Buffaloes, together.

Today the number of Darwin clubs accepting players from all walks of life has multiplied, making football appear the great equaliser. And when you know its local history, it is clear how football has helped to even the score.

3

Living it

Chromies, swampies and the kindness of strangers

Pulling in a fish after hours of patient scanning, some kind of soul transference happens. The more the fish fights, the more its human aggressor comes to life. There is a very private physical connection as killer and victim meet in opposition. Adrenaline threads its charge through formerly lax muscles, tightening everything as it goes. The heartbeat spikes, the tongue dries. Arms become springs, wound tight as the reel. The fish's refusal to die quietly is precisely what this now fully-charged human seeks. But of course it is seldom an equal match. As the fish takes its fight with the hook into anaerobic fields, lactic acid pumps through its flesh, changing the composition of its blood. It can die of this acid wash or suffocate slowly from a lethal clumping of its gills once it is hauled into air.

It makes it hard for those who like to fish, but not the threat of stock depletion, to catch and release a fish safely. But this is exactly what fishing expert Peter Zeroni teaches people to do: how to treat fish humanely in the act of hunting them for sport. He counsels circle hooks, barbless lures and no live bait. Yet caring does not erase the threat, even if one kisses the fish before dropping them back into the water.

I grew up with Peter Zeroni. We are the same age, give or take a few days; we were born in the same hospital; our mothers were in the same ward. From the earliest days of being able to write his name, Peter's signature came with a fish chasing a hook. It's an old joke between us that I've never gone fishing with him and he's never come swimming with me. So it is no surprise to learn that in our middle age he has a boat, *Barraddiction*, and a side career as a fishing writer and photographer, with an occasional newspaper column and a blog on the website Fishing World. He even snaps his own photographs, and though I view trophy shots with the same horror as an icefield of newly bludgeoned baby seals, his photos are things of wonder. Together we examine shots of fish thrashing between water and boat, light catching the halo of water drops; a fish mid-leap, still free, its inky eye fixed side-on to the lure, a hunter staring down its prey; and still lifes of someone grinning, holding a just-caught fish aloft in two hands, like a platter being offered to the viewer. He dismisses one such shot, shaking his head at my dutiful exclamations about the fish size. 'Pity it's just a swampie,' he says of the freshwater barra, its scales coated in green slime hinting at its muddy 'swamp dog' taste. The barramundi of choice is a 'chromie', its silver scales as shiny as a polished coat of armour, best caught in saltwater estuaries or out at sea.

We were yarning in Peter's office, which would be like any other public sector manager's room, with its whiteboard, filing cabinets and wood veneer round table for mini-meetings, but for the dazzling collection of lures decorating his

computer console and the fish portraits everywhere — hung, stockpiled or leaning against walls.
Each lure had a biography, a story of luck or mem-
orable adventure, and a technical history of purpose and craftsmanship. Fishing for Peter is life
itself. Of course, work is challenging and needs
to be meaningful, but, like a fish, pay-as-you-earn
jobs can be let go. In present-day Darwin, it's not
a bad philosophy. With respective governments
slashing public sector positions, nobody's job is
guaranteed. Fishing is a pastime, he tells me with
a laugh, that forgives ageing bodies, bad backs and
balding heads. Yet, while it can be done with next
to no equipment, a fortnightly refill of the wallet
sure helps. The more common form of fishing
involves boats, vehicles strong enough to tow them,
trailers, the ability to keep all of these registered,
ice, tackle, and fuel — lots of fuel. Rumour has it
that the average price of an amateur-caught catch
is at least $500 per fish. Perhaps this is why it is
hard for Darwin tourists to eat barra in a pub; half
the time they'll get Nile perch and be spun a line
that the barra isn't biting.

In between our reveries about Darwin pre- and
post-cyclone, Peter explains the pleasures of fishing
in terms that are at once self-deprecating, technical

and full of reverence. Fishing switches the world off. Fishers are drawn to the enforced solitude, the practice of listening to natural sounds, the plunk of water against a resting boat, the call of a sea eagle, the soft rustles of a breeze swishing canvas wraps. The sounds weave little dream worlds into the working person's fragmented time clock. Even the outboard engine plays its part. Like a lawn mower, it kills non-essential talk. Passengers concentrate on sensations instead – the play of light on water or the thump of cross-angling another boat's wake. The mind is alert yet relaxed. The hours of hunting in wait are almost as perfect as landing a catch.

Take Shady Camp, Peter tells me, describing a well-known fishing spot, named for its treelessness, over 200 kilometres' drive inland from Darwin in the Mary River National Park. 'There's no mobile coverage. There's run-off water travelling fast. There's tides. There's mud. There's sand bars. There are crocs, propellers, sharp hooks on lures and knives to worry about. You can't afford to be distracted. When you're there, you don't have time to think about extraneous things like your day job.'

Fishing takes you places you wouldn't otherwise

go to without a purpose and offers purposeless-
ness as reward. Later I meet Christina Hurren,
event coordinator of the annual Secret Women's
Business (SWB) Barra Challenge, and she agrees
with the general philosophy. It's that feeling of
being small and insignificant in a larger universe
which sets fishing, and for that matter, Darwin,
apart. Chrissie came to Darwin a few years ago.
As she stepped off the plane in the sultry October
heat, she knew immediately she had left Sydney's
eastern suburbs behind. Within two months she
met her future husband, a soldier who'd been relo-
cated to Darwin in the same month she'd arrived.
He introduced her to fishing. Both new to Darwin,
they would throw in a line to spend time together,
first off jetties in town, then further afield. A wedding gift of some of the finest fishing gear money
could buy stoked the fishing passion. She got an
army guy who drives semitrailers to teach her how
to reverse a trailer with flair. She learnt about
fishing tackle, how to treble a lure and knot lines
artfully; how to spot mullet movements (a sign of
other fish nearby); and, most importantly, how to
keep a fish hooked once it's taken the bait.

Fishing took her into Darwin's backyard, its
famed wilderness, the mangrove bowers and sharp

pandanus. She saw wading birds standing in vigil on open water plains and bent trees with branches draped over water. They'd take off so ponderously, spindly legs scratching at the air as if they'd forgotten how to lift, before stretching up and out with such supreme mastery their watchers become the graceless ones. Far from disliking feelings of insignificance, fishers like Pete and Chrissie seem to revel in the humbling. Sitting vulnerable in boats, with legionnaire caps and neck buffs, long-sleeved shirts and sunglasses as shields, sensing the immensity of the universe and the puniness of people is strangely gratifying. One time Chrissie was casting a line when an eagle stole the bait off her hook as it arced through the air, a brazen rush of wings, beak and talons. 'It was the most incredible thing I have ever seen in my life.' The haunting red gleam of crocodile eyes by torchlight has a similar subduing effect.

With over one in five non-Indigenous residents in Darwin admitting they had gone fishing at least once over the latest survey year; and with the majority fishing from privately owned boats in the Darwin harbour region and surrounds, it is with good reason that Darwin is hailed as the capital of recreational fishing in Australia. A government-issued pamphlet on the few fishing controls that exist equates 'recreational fishing' and 'the great Territory lifestyle' three times in its opening pages, and they know what they mean by it, for fishing with relative impunity is synonymous with Top End citizenship. It is this collective sense of entitlement which sees politicians bowing to the demands of the Amateur Fishermen's Association of the Northern Territory, AFANT. The fishing trip can be an unwalled meeting venue, where development decisions and business deals are made in relaxed and unrecorded surrounds. Darwin's generous supply of boat ramps and access roads are one outcome; fishing villas for members of political parties another. The bumper stickers 'I fish and I vote' and 'I boat, float and vote' warn of the influential men and women who fish the estuaries and shores, from jetties and boats, facing an incoming tide or searching out snags and gutters, with lures, live bait, nets, traps, alone or in groups, to while away an evening or focus an organised multi-day trip, fishing for mud crabs, bream, jewfish, coral trout, golden snapper and, most of all, for barramundi.

The chin-wagging banter of *Tales from the Tinny* — a Saturday morning ABC radio show which welcomes the weekend with fishing swagger – belies the power and influence of the angling community. But for anyone who wants to be elected or to stay elected in Darwin, the fishing lobby matters. This, then, is the background to the vigorous local reaction to the High Court of Australia's 2008 Blue Mud Bay decision. The ruling basically extended the title that Aboriginal Land Trusts had gained under the *Aboriginal Land Rights (NT) Act* 1976 (Cth) to bits of the once unbroken Aboriginal estate. To enter these intertidal waters, both commercial and recreational fishers now need a permit or permission from traditional owners, who can veto access altogether. It concerns some 80 per cent of the Territory coastline, the rugged, 'real' Territory of frontier dreams.

The moment the Blue Mud Bay decision was announced, the government became hysterically obsessed with guaranteeing as much 'permit-free' (that is, fee-free) access to popular recreational fishing areas as it could negotiate, preferably in perpetuity, offering development bribes and concessions on other gridlocked issues (such as forestalling deep-sea mining) as sweeteners. In this ongoing negotiation, AFANT's concern about being 'locked out' of popular fishing spots is shared, with greater vitriol, by letter writers, talkback radio callers and bloggers. As 'Mike' of Stuart Park puts it: 'Waterways are meant to be for the public. Perhaps if they [the traditional owners] want to go private they can fund their homes and health clinics that the public provide too!'

The explosive politics are no new thing in Darwin – rage over itinerants, public drunkenness, or seemingly generous government spending programs animates the local airwaves just as routinely – but there can be tricky alliances too. Fishers prefer aquatic habitats to be maintained or restored to improve fish catch prospects, particularly in the breeding areas, and have strong attachments to areas where good fishing can still be had. When valued waterways like the Roper or Daly Rivers come under threat from mining or agricultural pursuits, AFANT speaks in concert with the Land Councils, environmental activists and Indigenous resource managers. Its members have successfully campaigned to reduce licences for commercial fishing (even banning commercial boats from the entire Darwin Harbour region)

and are ever-vigilant about aquatic invasive species. Yet anglers are not as innocent of environmental damage as the sector's advocacy efforts
might imply. Just as fishers can contain the contradiction between caring for fish and wanting to bag
them, so too they can have ethics about aquatic
worlds yet remain one of the threats to be managed. Recreational catch data is incomplete (how
much barramundi is caught is not disaggregated),
but there are clear pressures on the more easily
accessed fishing sites in and around Darwin.

Such regulations as exist have only rudimen-
tary enforcement. The mortality levels from catch
and release methods are poorly researched, while
the pollution generated by fishing (from discarded
fishing lines through to plastic bags, drink cans
and beer bottles) is not considered a serious threat.
Fishers are simply exhorted to take care with their
rubbish, but are not penalised for the deaths or
injuries caused by their detritus. It falls to Darwin
artist Aly de Groot, weaving sea creatures from
ghost nets and discarded lines, to properly describe
the impact. She weaves jellyfish sculptures to tell
a story about the turtles drowned by nets – nets
which keep on fishing long after they've been discarded – and how turtles die of toxic poisons when

they eat plastic bags, mistaking them for their preferred diet of jellyfish. Without turtles and other predators, and buoyed by the warming acidity of an increasingly seasick environment, jellyfish are thriving.

The modern day angler must embrace many contradictions in their desire to be at one with nature. They might learn the language of tides and exalt in the lessons of clouds, but they will arm themselves with precision GPS technology and echo sounders to locate and track their hunt.

In the midst of these troublesome waters is the valuable saltwater barramundi, the most targeted fish in the Northern Territory. They are the kings and queens of the recreational fishing world, delicious to eat and thrilling to catch, fighting the line all the way and clever in spitting out hooks. Pursuing barramundi sees fishers chasing the run-offs from the first rains of the reviled build-up period, for this is when the barra spawns amid the saltwater shallows of river mouths and bays. Juvenile barras then surf the high spring tides into mangroves and wetland habitats, feasting on mozzie larvae and just about anything else they find in the swamps and tides. From there they migrate further upriver, taking up residence in freshwater enclaves as the wet season shrinks the wetlands, emerging three or more years later to head back out to salt water for spawning. They are what is known as protandrous hermaphrodites, meaning they start life as males and change into females upon maturity. Salt water is needed for this transformation: barramundi bred in isolated freshwater lagoons can grow large all right, but will stay male. Under normal conditions, not only is the barramundi promiscuous, he becomes she and, if there are too many females, she can become he again. Generally, the smaller fish (less than 70 to 80 centimetres) are almost always male; larger fish, including the prized 'metrey' (100 centimetres or more), are almost always female.

The way Peter Zeroni tells it, the 'metrey' is an honourable quarry. The fisher should praise this breeder and not pull her out of the water at all, or else hold her carefully, horizontally, for just as long as it takes to get a weighing and a photograph, before releasing it in less than a couple of minutes — about the same time it takes for the human brain to suffer damage when it is oxygen deprived. It would be a mongrel act to dangle such a fish vertically, tearing its internal organs apart or dislocating its jaw and spine, surefire ways of gifting it a tortured death if placed back in the water. A bloke boasting of keeping a large chromie would infuriate knowledgeable anglers and be hounded for his cavalier disregard. After all these years, Peter can be lost in the uncanny stare of a barramundi's eyes, but the beauty of the fish is not the point. A breeding female is too valuable to be caught just the once. She needs to be recycled.

The political power of angling lobbyists combines multiple contradictions. The angling community's sheer numbers and diversity makes it difficult to isolate them as a discrete demographic grouping, for fishers are just as likely to be conservationists as they are to be conservative party voters. And while fishing is something that is mostly done by young to middle-aged men, bonding fathers and sons, brothers and mates, it involves a growing number of women and children, using traditions passed down generational lines.

Chrissie Hurren enjoys the family-oriented nature of fishing, but in the Secret Women's Business Barra Challenge that she coordinates, the rules are simple: no men, no children, no pollution. Competitors spend two days at Corroboree Billabong, where they catch, measure and release

the barramundi, saratoga and tarpon they are targeting. It is as competitive or frivolous as participants want it to be, but for SWB organisers it has
a serious dimension. They have worked hard to
achieve a 4.5 from 5 star ranking from NEATFish
(National Environmental Assessment of Tourna-
ment Fishing), which measures SWB's processes
for minimising detrimental impacts on fish
stocks; being environmentally sustainable; gar-
nering support from, and providing positive social
and economic benefits to, local communities; and
offering safe fishing experiences for competitors
and spectators alike. Women of all skill levels are
welcome. Some participants train intensely for
the event, go to bed early and hit the water before
dawn to bag the best hauls; others party hysterically, decorate themselves and their boats, and
drink champagne from sun-up to sundown, gig-
gling as they cast their lines. There are entertain-
ments, activities, fun and serious prizes (champion
team, best-dressed boat). No men are allowed, not
even as boat skippers, and anyone caught littering
suffers instant disqualification.

We could be forgiven for thinking that coordi-
nating this female empowerment event, finding her
life partner and becoming an accomplished fisher

are what explains Chrissie's feeling that Darwin is home forever. But paradoxically it was the loss of her home that showed her why she needed to stay. It started with flames springing to life from a toaster in the kitchen on 19 July 2012. Chrissie was at work, her young son at home with his Nan, playing happily with toys. The fire alarm sounded, the fire department arrived at speed, and no one was hurt. But everything was lost: burnt to charcoal, ruined by smoke, blasted by water. James's baby book survived, with burn marks on the cover, an extraordinary memento, but Darwin's lesson remains true: things don't matter. 'No one was hurt. We could get on with life because we were all still together.'

The laughter we'd been sharing as we likened tackle boxes to sewing kits – all little drawers and favourite knick-knacks – has been swallowed by the pain of slowed-down sentences, but Chrissie needs to tell this, to truly explain what Darwin now means to her. That drive home was the longest of her life. Arriving at her street in the Defence housing suburb of Lyons, the smoke belching from her house sped her past onlookers and the police barricade. Someone tried to stop her; she shunted them aside. Television reporters greeted her with microphones. Her biggest regret was talking to them. 'I wanted them to go away. I thought by talking to them I would make that happen. But it didn't.'

I could hear the confusing clamour from the wince of her eyes, the catch in her breath as she tells the story. She pantomimes with her body: twisting her torso and holding up her hands to show how she'd looked to the police, then to her sister, back to the journalists, seeking guidance. 'What do I do? I don't know. I don't know.' She talked to the media in a daze and watched in horror as the story went live. Channel Nine broke the news with a story that laid the blame on their toddler and his negligent carers.

As army personnel, the Defence Department immediately organised replacement accommodation, but the family had nothing to put in it. Then the most remarkable turn of events. Complete strangers gave them money, grocery vouchers, a bag of toys. A Tupperware consultant organised a fundraiser, a Facebook appeal was started and yet more strangers signed up to help. People turned up at the house with carloads of cutlery, glasses, bed sheets. Embarrassed at all the unbidden charity, Chrissie protested 'but we have insurance'. Her donors brushed her away, reminding her that right now she needed their help. Hard as it was to admit, they were right. It was a strange and alienating time, to suddenly become 'the someone else' that these things happen to. She heard with flat detachment the Territory Insurance Office annual statistics that there'd been four catastrophic house fires that year, knowing their home was one of the listed four, yet unable to feel any vital connection to this fact. But it was this ordeal by fire, the forced shift from being fiercely independent, handy with trailers and heaving fish, to relying on the kindness of strangers, which affirmed why Darwin should be called home.

Heritage and rubble

The people of post-war Darwin shared one great love: the Hotel Darwin. Opened for business in 1940 on the corner of Herbert Street and the Esplanade, it was both excitingly modern and raffishly old, a key part of the town's social geography. Its palm-studded lawns, shaded verandahs, wooden casement windows and 'distinctive canopy of blue Marseilles tiles' gave it the film noir effect of a colonial building in a tropical savanna. With its all-white exterior, it was Darwin's version of Singapore's Raffles Hotel, a place of escape and fantasy. Visiting dignitaries were taken there to be specially impressed by what the little frontier town had to offer. It promised intimacy in a world of heartbeats and pheromones heightened by the heat. Soldiers drank at the hotel bar and courted willing nurses. Civilians would dress in their best and steal glances, testing for the frisson that might lead to something more. Then, with the flick of a drummer's wrist, the drama of a joyfully bellowed argument, people leaning into each other to hurl points against the noise. A drunken kind of candour joined the male politicians, public servants and journalists in the hotel's main lounge, the Green Room, long socks and short-sleeved shirts contrasting with the jungle foliage cushions of their colonial cane chairs.

Known affectionately as 'the Grand Old Duchess' for its extraordinary charm, its near overnight demolition in September 1999 still claws at people's memories. In next to no time, piles of rubble stood in the place of a hotel whose lovely art deco visage had formerly graced postcards of Darwin, suggesting the sound of jazz music and the heady scent of frangipani. In its place, the clearly impermanent Palms City Resort, cloned cabin pods offering convenient town accommodation in a tropical setting, furnished with tasteful yet removable fittings.

People were furious, heartbroken, bewildered. Their beloved hotel had survived bombs and cyclones only to be destroyed by its owners, the Paspalis hotel group, one week before it was due to be reconsidered for listing on the NT Heritage Register, which would theoretically protect it. The destruction of the hotel came to symbolise everything that was maddening about Darwin: its rampant developmentalism; the unimportance of history to the transient population; the environmental hostility to significant structures; the cowboy politics. It was the sort of thing that could only happen in Darwin, people lamented. A symbol of the erosion of Darwin's core values; another attack on its fast-vanishing distinction.

Members of the National Trust had tried to stop the demolition, successfully seeking a Supreme Court injunction. The injunction was granted on Monday 8 September. Next day, Justice Stephen Bailey had it overturned. Another source of rescue was still possible. Mike Reed, then acting Minister for Conservation, could have asserted his powers under the *Heritage Conservation Act* and issued an interim conservation order to stall the demolition for a further ninety days. He chose not to. The public outcry was never going to move him, for this was a man who courted controversy. Another day, Reed woke up and arbitrarily decided to axe the Territory's funding for bilingual education programs in remote schools, the only bit of non-Commonwealth funding the Territory government used to put into Indigenous education. Community anger over the Darwin Hotel was water off Reed's back. The demolition sped ahead.

Ironically, it was Minister Reed who had introduced the Heritage Conservation Bill in 1991, the first formalisation of heritage protection in the Territory's history. But when the Bill was actually used by the pesky National Trust to prevent demolition of the old Alice Springs jail, the government responded in characteristic form, passing an amendment which essentially gave a minister the ability to damage, destroy, demolish, desecrate or remove a heritage place or object, the drafters scouring the thesaurus for synonyms as they scribed the new legislative powers. Even better, where usually public projects or private development contracts signed off by local authorities endure at least nominal rituals of transparency, when it comes to demolishing a heritage-listed item, the minister need give no reasons at all.

It proved an addictive amendment, a rare gift of rigmarole-free ministerial powers. (After all, the key reason Mal Brough chose to command the Australian Defence Force to execute the Northern Territory Emergency Response in 2007 was that it bypassed ordinary departmental palaver.) Of course, the same bureaucratic proceduralism that is sliced through by the heritage amendment has its uses. The incoming Labor government of 2001 spent such a long time reviewing, consulting and issuing reports on how the Territory's non-heritage legislation might be revised, they lost incumbency before changing much at all.

With no last-minute stay of execution from Minister Reed, heavy bulldozers worked overnight on Friday 12 September 1999. By the time people arrived for work on Monday, there was nothing left to save.

The Paspalis company claimed an engineering report had identified concrete cancer in the building, which would have cost untold millions to salvage. But where the company argued a natural inevitability, the public sniffed pursuit of a business profit. There were at least two engineering reports at the time the Hotel Darwin was felled, the one waved around by the Paspalis, suggesting enormous works were at stake, and another suggesting the opposite. Builders and engineers who spoke to historian David Carment immediately after the demolition were among those suggesting minor repairs. The old Hotel Darwin was one of three sites shortlisted for the construction of a new 1500-seat convention and exhibition centre. Eight months after the hotel's demolition, the Hotel Darwin site was elevated to number one preference and the Paspalis company won the right to negotiate with the government on how the centre would be constructed. The Paspalis envisioned a two-tower hotel on top of the convention centre, subsidised by the government – which is when negotiations faltered. In the end, twelve years after the wrecking of the Grand Old Duchess, the new Convention Centre was built at a different site altogether, and by a different government.

The keen loss felt by Darwinites over the Hotel Darwin is easy to understand. If architectural dynasties define a city, then Darwin's nostalgia hovers over rare pickings. Even without multiple destructions, there are few legacies of former wealth and grandeur, for dreamers with the money to build with future prosperity in mind were always few and far between. Their impact, when they did come, was always large in local eyes.

In 1931, when the golf- and horserace-loving Tom Harris arrived in Darwin at the age of thirty-four, the place was still a raw frontier town. Everything was freighted in, Darwin's military status was only half-decided, the roads were unsealed, racial laws targeting Chinese and Aborigines were in full swing and dirt-poor peanut farmers were starving out on the Daly River plains. The jaunty Victorian raconteur had come to manage the fledgling Star Theatre on the recommendation of his brother, John, a solicitor who, having lost his leg in World War I, had set up practice in the frontier town some years prior. Tom's management intervention was critical. The Star had been bought as a going concern by a consortium of local investors and the team was losing money fast.

Almost instantly he began to see more than he had been expected to. There was the free-spirited Heather Bell, playing piano to build the mood for the silent action sequences, her red hair aglow with screen reflections. Darwin-born Heather had refused the hand of most of the eligible young men who had asked, for each had failed her test: were they prepared to stay in Darwin? She was not the kind to waver. The same year Tom had arrived, she'd been fined in lieu of seven days imprisonment 'for using the Darwin baths without first paying the usual fee. Defendant was twice sent notice to pay but did not do so.' Pursuing feisty Heather by proving good his Darwin commitment was one goal. By the time their son Tom, then their grandson Tom Harris were born as Darwin boys, Heather was convinced.

Then there was the picture theatre. Old Tom envisioned it as a site for social functions, masquerade dances, plays, community benefit nights, impromptu cabarets, music and singing. Being a betting man from Victoria, he soon established the Tomaris Darwin Annual Melbourne Cup Sweep, 'Tomaris' for the sound that 'Tom' and 'Harris' make when run together, mashed lazily, Darwin-style. And he imagined a procession of people of all ethnicities coming to the Star to see the talkies, still a novelty in Sydney and Melbourne and not yet available up north.

Far from being a passive manager, for the next few months Tom worked first on having the business leased to him before eventually purchasing it outright. By 1933, less than two years after arriving, he showed the first talking picture. By the mid-1950s, the Star and the Hotel Darwin were the centres of entertainment in Darwin, and, in time, it made sense for the Harris family to join forces with the Paspalis family, who'd meantime started a rival picture theatre in Parap and opened Darwin's only drive-in picture theatre in Nightcliff. The Star Theatre thrived until the arrival of Darwin's first fully enclosed and fully air-conditioned cinema complex in Mitchell Street in the early 1970s. With the damage it sustained from Cyclone Tracy, its doors never reopened.

Tom senior's legendary open-heartedness helped him commercially navigate Darwin's apartheid race relations. Directly opposite the Four Birds courtyard cafe in the now revamped Star Village off the Smith Street Mall, an enlarged metal photograph is fixed to a wall. Taken in the 1930s, it reflects audience faces viewed from the stage. A number of people in the bottom rows closest to the viewfinder clench their eyes tightly shut, cover their faces with their hands, or turn aside completely. They are either guarding their eyes from the blinding flashlight, or, as the photograph's explanatory text has it, are convinced the camera will steal their souls. The photo also shows Darwin's status hierarchy: Aboriginal, Chinese and rough Anglos sit on the cheaper seats closest to the screen, under the stars and exposed to the elements, overlooked by more finely attired top-town Anglo-Celtics, enjoying deckchairs on the sheltered balustrade above the coloured fray.

The segregated seating did nothing to discourage patronage. During the Star's heyday, so many Aboriginal people demanded to attend Wednesday 'yippee' nights that the Northern Territory Chief Protector took to issuing group waivers from the town compounds for the evening. People would come dressed in their best pipe-seamed and tasselled shirts, workman jeans, decorated-buckle belts, akubra hats, spurs and boots. There were pastoralists, stockmen, owners and workers alike, going on benders before and after the show, spurring on the actors with their laughing and wailing, hoots and wisecracks. Policemen might work the crowd too, spotting warrant dodgers and curfew breakers, but mostly it was a night for circus revelry. It even attracted Hugh Wason Byers, the

tough man from Coolibah, as part of the celebrated talent when the motion picture *Jedda* had its
world premiere at the Star.

Jedda was not, as is popularly thought, Australia's first feature-length film shot in colour (the
film *Kangaroo* deserves that title), but it was among
the first to have Aboriginal actors playing the
Indigenous parts. The Chauvels had been warned
to use white professionals in black paint. 'Aborigines, they were told, "had the smallest brain box
of any human living"; they could not concentrate for more than 10 minutes; they would not
work from one day to the next but would go on
walkabout.' The Chauvels took the opposite tack,
reverting Rosalie Kunoth's name to Ngarla and
ignoring Robert Tudawali's common name of Bob
Wilson to further highlight the Aboriginality of
the film's stars. As it showed its story of racial
division and cultural difference, mirroring the
mix and splits of *Jedda*'s debut audience, Ngarla
and Tudawali were 'treated' to a viewing from the
Star Theatre balustrade.

The modern day Star Village has the cosmopolitan

feel of Melbourne's laneways and arcades, with a dedicated cafe, al fresco salad bar, designer and vintage clothing stores, a *chocolaterie*, and a restaurant boasting the best laksa in Darwin. The picture theatre's old projector sits at the entrance, together with a board listing the winners of the first Tomaris Sweep. First name on the board: Hugh Wason Byers. I think I am being haunted.

The laneway feel is not an accidental effect. The Star had been suffering Darwin's post-cyclone economic ups and downs, until 'young Tom' – now approaching fifty – set out to revitalise his family's business. Enduring the debt that came with it, Tom resisted leasing empty shops until he could attract tenants with something outside the ordinary. He gave artist and storyteller Wayne Lennox Miles ('Milesy') free reign to rummage through the Harris family archives, a treasure trove of original movie posters, photographs and old-timey theatre paraphernalia. Milesy created storyboards from the fascinating snippets to line the plaza, enlarging old photos for casual patron viewing. With its creative vibe restored, the precinct was recovering its origins as a gathering place, somewhere locals can greet each other and visitors can access a little of what Darwin is about. With the environmental and political threats to anything old, there are few such places left: the Frances Bay trailer boat, yacht and ski clubs; Dinah Beach yacht club; the beaches and picnic spots; and perhaps the old Railway Club in Parap are practically all that remain. Everything else is anonymously new, or so hidden it has to be known and shown. After all, modern-day Darwin is occupied by (mostly) men in the mining industry and Defence Forces, new immigrant groups from Africa and workers from Ireland, community gardeners committed to organic produce and athletic women playing high-speed roller derby at Marrara Stadium.

Managing the Star is only one of Tom's business responsibilities, yet somehow we find time to meet between his multiple appointments and my Darwin–Sydney sojourns. But instead of showcasing the Village, he elects to meet at the Boatshed Coffee House, a cafe down at Cullen Bay Marina, directing my gaze to the decor. The servery is made of rehabilitated ship timbers, mini orb and anchor ropes. On the walls are collages of photographs and found objects, telling stories of human–sea interactions in and around Darwin. He will take me to meet the creator, Milesy, another time. At this meeting we cover the history of the famous picture house. Tom opens a binder he's about to loan me, a collection of Star memorabilia from its early days as an open-air theatre to now.

'You'll like this one,' he says, slowing the page-turning. It is a newspaper story about when his grandfather installed a mini putt-putt course in the theatre, with Colonel Weddell, the Resident Administrator, competing in the first match. He reads another excerpt, from 1995. Chief Minister Shane Stone was describing Tom's grandmother Heather Bell during his maiden speech to parliament. Heather had been evacuated after the bombing, but husband Tom senior had stayed behind to run the picture theatre and entertain the troops. Hubby was summonsed with a letter, young Tom reads aloud, mimicking Shane Stone's voice, 'which bluntly commanded "If you don't get down here soon, there will be another bull in the paddock!"'

We laugh, and I remember that Tom's father was an elected member representing the Port of Darwin. It had been his resignation that gave Stone his portal into Territory politics. It makes sense of the young Tom before me, who is fully *au fait* with Territory politics despite a declared impatience with the topic. But it is as a landlord that he corrects popular stories about the Hotel

Darwin. Tom shares my love of ceiling fans and timber decks, and joins my lament about the loss of louvred, elevated houses in today's suburban estates and austere high-rise complexes, but he is less sentimental about that old hotel's fate.

For all that the Star's transformation is a proud achievement, keeping it going takes more than nostalgia. The building was originally made from local materials. Today, its old stones are brittle as chalk, mortared with cement made from beach sand, still full of salt and crumbling back into single grains. Driven by sentiment, Tom spent a fortune on scaffolding and reinforcements, to the point of financial recklessness. 'We're done,' he says, on the question of maintaining the site in the future.

'People say of the Star "Oh, it looks fantastic", but there's a bucketload of money sitting inside that steel. And we don't get any return on it.

'People have to look at heritage a little bit differently,' Tom continues, warming to the subject with the help of a second coffee. 'Private owners can't expect to maintain a building that's falling down when they didn't buy buildings to be heritage originally and there's no public money available to support our salvation efforts.

'These old buildings were reinforced back in the day, but that was 80-odd years ago, with a product that's got salt in it, and with our wet seasons ... The Paspalis survived Cyclone Tracy, but an area of the hotel was busted off. We had bits knocked off our building too. So any little crack, water gets in. You wouldn't need a lot. The reinforcements expand, it blows the concrete, lets more water in, corrodes the mortar.'

As the walls sucked in rainwater, forcing bricks and mortar to loosen their once tight embrace, each new striation forged a sweaty corrosion path, so delicate yet sure that even the muscle-strong girders and joists began to anticipate their own destruction.

'Look, the Paspalis might have got a few more years out of the Hotel Darwin, but it wouldn't've gone on forever. They would have had to encase the whole thing in a new concrete skin and reinforce the skeletal structure, lost their ceiling height and, with that, a lot of the original feel. Maybe they could've retained some of the facade – big emphasis on the *maybe* – but it'd gone beyond its life.'

I am inclined to believe him. As I've learnt from long anthropological immersion in the built forms of remote Australia, the true horrors of renovation are never known until a building's fabric has been pulled aside. It is then that its support structures are revealed in all their termite-riddled, rust-corroded, death-trap glory. The look of a thing is almost always deceptive, like Darwin itself. It's that old Darwin story again, this place that lures people in and spits on their possessions. Bits of Darwin's essence might be retained in protected buildings, but it's just as authentically traced in the quick-build replacements. As ancient and ephemeral, as resilient and vulnerable as ever.

Eating warm mangoes

When I finally meet the wiry, wary artist Wayne Lennox Miles, visual architect of the Star Village's revival, I feel I already know him. This is Darwin all over. There's total strangers, known familiars and a whole bunch of folk sparking your memory in uncatchable ways. Wayne's workshop, the Tin Shed Gallery in Coconut Grove, is filled with the colours and textures of his home town. It is a gleaner's trove, non-air-conditioned, eclectic. Shelves groan with curios and natural harvests — seashells, bits of driftwood — winnowed from the fringe of plastic bottles and esky foam lining the city's beachfronts.

There are sculptural pieces, buffalo heads fashioned from real horns and metal sheeting, rusted to the colour of a tanned hide; found-object artworks; photographs. A coffee table straddles a woven pandanus circle-mat and offers up a bowl filled with green, mustard and milky-white glass pebbles, from old beer bottles tossed to sea over years beyond count, softened by sand-grind. The shed screeches with typical Darwin noises too, from men working at a commissioned art piece with welders and circular saws. Sparks fly over our heads as we duck into his office, a respite of stacked papers and creative bric-a-brac.

Over the whine of tools and work-cussing, Wayne sets the ball rolling on what makes a Darwinite. At first he tells me something I already accept: that for a large part of its settlement history the Territory was based around stock and the men who, trained as shooters in the race wars of home and abroad, 'basically went into the shooting business – cattle or buffalo shooting or crocodile hunting or pearl-shell grabbing, pet-meaters, all those sorts of things'. Before all those men died or got too old to tell their stories, Wayne spent time with them, gathering their life stories and taking photographs. He has even heard of Hugh Wason Byers.

'They inevitably went out to bush and had lubras for wives, gins — that's what they'd call them — because realistically not many white women would put up with the conditions. Because those places were tough. It wasn't like watching a *Crocodile Dundee* movie. It was *for real*, mate. It was *full* of mosquitoes. If you got a cut on your leg in the wet season, it'd fester up. The food was *shit*.' These black women are not popularly celebrated as pioneers of the land though, we agree, thinking about glossy depictions of heroic outback women in pale brushed-cotton jeans and tailored bush shirts. I guess it's the defining right of those who declare sovereignty over others to also remember its enforcers in reverential terms.

Those shooters gave us the mixed-up population that Darwinites refer to with such affection, its treasured multiculturalism, Wayne points out; but he also remembers the dividing lines amid the easy pluralism.

'You know, I grew up in that environment, whites and blacks together in Darwin. We were segregated, there was no doubt about it, even at the Star Village, where the whitefellas used to sit upstairs and blackfellas sit downstairs. They say it was to do with the price of the tickets, but there was way more to it than that.'

At primary school Wayne learnt how to fight, kiss girls and smoke. Later, he'd wag school and hang out in storage sheds, pounding stockpiles of asbestos fibreboard into powdery debris for the hell of it. And – deepest education of all – he understood how to navigate the colour codes ordering the streets, buses and schoolyards, using fists, alcohol, hunting and sporting prowess. Listening to him, it is as if being a Darwinite means knowing the unspoken lores and dingo-lingo of an exotic anthropological fieldsite, mastered through full-body immersion.

But the definition of a Darwinite doesn't settle here. It is a debate that uses exclusion criteria as shifty as the town's turbulent demographics. Contests over the title take place every day, in every rebuttal in letters and texts to the *NT News*, in every protest about a tightening of rules where before there were none. Disconnecting drinking alcohol from driving a vehicle, having speed limits, or suggesting fireworks should be illegal invoke the rallying cry: Go back to where you came from! You're not a local!

For some, a Darwinite must have been born in Darwin; for others, they must have lived in the town before Cyclone Tracy came and blew it away. Growing up to the songs of garage band The Swamp Jockeys might be a marker, as could preferring Paul's Iced Coffee over other flavoured milk brands. Perhaps it is being old enough to have snuck into the Nightcliff Drive-in, coiled like a carpet snake in someone's boot. Or remembering the time when people viewed the Beer Can Regatta as a clever re-use of the ugly drinkers' middens that use to line the Stuart Highway, a unique heraldry to announce the capital city.

Oftentimes, 'Darwinite' veers close in meaning to the term 'Territorian', a word adroitly wielded by the long ascendant Country Liberal Party as part of its divide-and-rule tactics. As David Carment writes, Territorianism was 'an aggressively presented sense of identity that encompassed full statehood and rapid economic development'. Criticism of Canberra was an essential feature, as was dutiful optimism about Darwin's promise as the gateway to trade with Asia. Somehow a Territorian was never Indigenous.

A Darwinite might not be someone who knows everyone, either. It is easily possible for old-timers and visitors returning after a twenty-year absence to be foreigners to modern-day Darwin. When the veteran journalist Tony Clifton returned to reassess Darwin's status as Australia's last frontier town, his verdict was negative. Darwin, he lamented, was no longer a place of hellraisers and pub brawls. It had become dull, 'a white-bread, nature-stripped, inward-looking, neat and clean haven for southern white migrants, who labour mainly in the coalmines of the NT administration and its sub-branches'.

Easy as it is to agree that the old frontier Darwin has disappeared, it is not quite true. There's no shortage of grizzled characters, eccentrics, beer bellies and beards. Beneath the veneer of development success stories lie pockets of terrible poverty, homelessness, alcoholism, violence, and a dormant racism that, like the melioidosis bacterium, sits a mere 10 centimetres below the surface. If anything, retailers say things are getting worse, bewailing the drunken fights choreographed outside their businesses and the human faeces they hose away each morning.

For Aboriginal visitors, Darwin has changed too, for good and bad. Once, you easily could come into town to get sly grog, heading to the small, tree-lined oasis known as One Mile Dam and other fringe camps, easily escaping public scrutiny. 'That's where all the visitors went, so many tribes,' my friends tell me. 'All dat family from Belyuen-Wadjigiyn, Kiyuk, all the tribes, long time ago, they used to go there, get flagon. Nobody hassled us in the old times. A long time ago, you could drink outside. Now we just get hassle. We just go there quick and come back.'

It is true, the place has changed. New Darwin finds its centre in Palmerston, the satellite town that is fast becoming the north's demographic centre, making the old peninsular CBD but one node, kept alive by public sector administrations, a 'golden mile' of pubs and nightclubs on Mitchell Street and a fierce rental market for serviced apartments. The city is no longer red dust interspersed with hand-watered patches of grass, but a more uniform green, courtesy of Australia's highest water consumption rates. There are more cafes and retail outlets, a convention centre, a wave pool, bike paths and, famously, assorted markets with their south-east Asian foodstuffs and bohemian feel. Houses meet the boundaries of their yards with more affluent conviction. A greater number of enclosed shopping malls and high-end retail outlets stand ready to satisfy consumer cravings. There is even a nightclub, Throb, celebrating cross-dressing and multiple sexualities – a far cry from the thrills and spills of Darwin's 'prawn and porn' nights (they've had to migrate further down the track). *ResideNT*, an up-market magazine issued by Throb's owners, portrays Darwin through the prism of local celebrities, all gourmet tastes and designer dazzle, so beautiful it is almost unrecognisable.

Yet some things haven't changed much at all. Describing a contemporary version of Milesy's old stomping grounds, for young people Darwin continues to have the attractions and the downsides of a large country town. 'You endure the heat, you get drunk. If you stay, you can have a baby and maybe get a home loan. It's better to get out,' one young man told me, briefly back home from his studies 'down south'. It can feel suffocating.

Lisa, who self-identifies as 'Eurasian', gave a similar verdict. 'It becomes very repetitive in Darwin after a while,' she told me. 'There's a strong culture of drinking and drug-taking. Everyone in Darwin's smoked weed or drunk crazy amounts of alcohol by age fifteen. It's more accepted there, more expected.

'And for people who are reasonably intelligent,

who are holding down jobs, their duty is to save up for a car or house or to start having their kids, not to dream of another life of creativity or adventure. Darwin makes you want to make security and permanence your priority.'

She paused, wanting to pinpoint what it is that drives young people out of Darwin or, if they stay, sorts them into binge drinkers or sturdy conservatives.

'There's a bit of a struggle for Darwin people to define their own identity – it gets fixed for you. You're a "tradie"', Lisa says, tagging the air with quote marks. 'Or an "AJ", a "Parmo-slut", whatever. If you want to escape it, you have to go down south, and then you can have a range of identities, no problem.'

AJs are 'Army Jerks' (though soldiers counterclaim it means Army Jocks). I had learnt about them from Donna, another Darwin-born girl from the post-cyclone generation. Donna never wants to leave. A trained jilleroo, she competes in rodeos, rides the mechanical bull in pubs to win free drinks and holds her own if a fight is on. She likes to shoot kangaroos, pigs and magpie geese and camp rough on long fishing trips. If anything, for Donna, Darwin has changed too much, become far too trendy. To find the type of blokey bloke and sense of 'old Darwin' she prefers, she heads to the bolted steel-frame corrugated iron pubs south of Darwin's Berrimah line.

'The clubs in town are too expensive,' she complains, 'and they're full of AJs, all out for a root and boot. The only part that's fun about those army boys is their pick-up lines and the professions they make up to avoid telling you they're army.' She laughs as she hurls her ute around another corner, with me wishing she'd change down a gear and find the brake pedal.

The young women have mapped out an entire sexual topography of Darwin and its transient menfolk. RAAF fellas are different, they tell me. They're after commitment. You can find them at certain clubs. But if you want quick sex with a buff AJ boasting a neat haircut and a decent apartment, you head to other clubs. AJs earn good money and, commanded to 'get in, get off, get out', will enjoy the drill. I am jealous and proud and horrified, all at once. This is new Darwin, with new sexual politics; and old Darwin, when teenagers had seedy trysts at East Point, and cruised back and forth between Shell 24 Hour at the airport gates, the wharf and Uncle Sam's.

Listening to Lisa and her friends, I thought of the paradox of Darwin, the puzzle of where it is and why it is. Here is a town with every reason to be the most different capital city in Australia and yet, in development terms, it's the most conventional. In many ways, it is a city like any other, with hotels that overcharge, inflated prices for tourist tat, franchised food outlets, big box retail zones, designed housing estates and look-alike high-rise buildings serving similar clientele: public servants, elite consultants and sojourning workers. Perhaps the chain wire fencing encircling building yards is meaner, the floodlights more menacing. Maybe there's more guard dogs and security company signs warning about patrolled premises, but that's hardly outstanding. New Darwin, the girls tell me, is found on the last public bus leaving from Mindil Beach markets, drunken men pissing on passenger seats as tipsy women squeal. Old Darwin had a lot of this too.

So what explains people's strong sense of Darwin's distinction? Locals talk of the 'lifestyle', but often as not this is code for middle-class comforts (air-conditioning, plentiful alcohol, seafood platters and giant flat screen TVs) and weekend toys: boats, jet skis and quad bikes. The incomes are higher here and there's more uncluttered space to rev engines. Joy is sought in consumption, the same as anywhere. And yet, there truly is something unique about Darwin. It is the smallest capital city in Australia, the least populated and least well known, no bigger than a country town, in the third-largest jurisdiction in Australia. It has the highest proportion of Indigenous population of any State or Territory: Aboriginal people are a defining political force and everyday presence. But what makes the town distinct goes beyond demographic differences. It is more elemental than brands of flavoured milk. Darwin is a place where confrontations with wild nature are not occasional and freakish, but perennial and expected. This matters.

Take the easily lampooned obsession with crocodiles, reliable source of front-page headlines for the local *NT News*, honoured and feared in equal measure. A crocodile aquarium in the central business district accepts a hefty fee to immerse caged visitors into a tank for photo opportunities with the world's largest living reptile. Yet, despite the hyperbole, they are a genuine part of the land-scape, our lions in the jungle. They thrive on fish, birds, livestock, pets and people, and turn up in the most unexpected places.

A few years ago, I went to the swimming pool at Nightcliff early in the morning, before the sun had come up. Let me tell you, Nightcliff Pool is truly one of the town's hidden secrets — but not because of its design. Like all Darwin's public pools, it is not built to competition standard. In fact, it is unusually shallow, which means it warms more readily in the build-up heat to a pea soup temperature, just when people are mad keen to escape the seething heat; and it cools more quickly in the dry, rapidly becoming far too cold for locals. Green sail cloths shading part of the pool give equally partial relief: one goes from dim to blinding light and back again, a different means of pacing each 50-metre sentence. The pool has old drainage and guttering systems and narrow lanes, so even if you are explosively fit, it still swims slow. It lacks the cubic hauling power of a sleekly designed contemporary aqua centre. At times, Nightcliff is so heavily doused in chlorine to ward off tropical festers it's like having your mouth swabbed with green banana skins.

So it is not by the crisp swimming that the pool bewitches. Its allure lies in its secret invitation to linger and drift, so rare in open-sun Darwin settings. With three sides of the pool facing the sea, people are happy to lay down a towel and read, ease into half-sleep or gambol in the water, the pool somehow summoning adults back to the joys of child play.

But that pearly dawn when I turned up for a swim, the prickly casuarina trees on the cliff edges still soft grey silhouettes, Nightcliff's sleepy rhythms had been disturbed. A saltwater crocodile measuring 1.6 metres had glued itself still against the bottom. There had been a heavy storm the night before, on a full tide. Another piece of Darwin magic: the storm at high tide. Waves crash into cliffs, clawing at the fragile barrier between land and sea, sending salty manes of water high into the air, spiking roads and paths with razor-sharp palm fronds. It is good stuff to get soaked in. Dangerous too, sweeping the unwary off rocks as swiftly as it shoots shrapnel in.

The little saltie had been thrown up onto a cliff ledge sometime during the night. It must have scrambled through the wire fencing around the pool, or perhaps it was given human help, as a lark, since croc-taunting has become something of a Top End pastime in recent years. When swim squad children turned up for their training session in the early morning, the animal sprinted across the lawn and bolted into the pool, where it stayed, petrified and wary, made smaller by the refraction of the water, no murky depths to disappear into, no hiding from the increasingly harsh light, until Parks and Wildlife Service rangers could organise a rescue two hours later.

The chlorine would have tasted foul to the wild creature. It tastes foul to me, and I know what I'm in for.

Darwin is a place that needs to be felt to be known. Its attractions are as primal as the dank smell of mould; as seductive as the mercury slipperiness of fresh spring-fed water, the honey of leaves bedded in streams so clear, so shimmeringly fresh, you can drink as you swim. It is the scent of freshly mown grass in the Wet Season, clumped in steaming piles, cut wet between downpours. Of steam rising from a hot road after a shower, the smell of dust and vaporous heat a welcome portent of more rain to come. It is lukewarm water from taps marked cold, the metallic fridge taste of foods kept safe from brazen rats the size of bricks, ants of every variety, weevils and cockroaches. The hint of smoke in the air hailing the Dry Season as surely as dragonflies darting through their hunting dance, the smoke wisps promising camping weather and bonfires. Swirls of cream, caramel, port wine and crimson in soft chalk rocks, fallen from eroding cliff faces. Bats screeching as they argue about fruit, then disintegrating on electricity lines. And, as reliable as the build-up, a beckoning sea that repels human entry by order of the lethal box jellyfish.

At the aching hour of lavender pinks and yellows when night greets day, dog walkers, joggers, cyclists, parents strolling their newborns emerge from their houses; they are joined at dusk by picnickers and fishers casting nets and lines. It is intimate and familial. Aboriginal campers are not so often snarled at in the gentling hours of sunrise and sunset. In the violent sunblast of day, tensions might resume, but still no one hurries. Men seldom wear ties and few bother with business suits — all cold-climate affectations. To walk Darwin-style is to slump the shoulders, drop the stomach muscles, sloth the foot tread. Thongs, sarongs and singlets take slow-moving bodies from shade into intense light, enervated by the force of sagging heat. It is bralessness without the politics. In the Dry Season, when the sky is hazy with smoke and dust, when the black kites are surfing the thermals and snatching insects from brushfires, when the winds blast dry leaves up into whirly-whirlies, the city comes alive. Streets and carparks fill with young backpackers from all over the world, and grey nomads hauling caravans from south-eastern Australia. Not for them the verdant growth and lightning shows of the Wet: they seek the joyous crackle of the Dry — smoke-enhanced sunsets and delicious market foods to help them forget winter's chill.

Later, when the festival season dies down, it's the pungent smell of mangoes left rotting where fruit bats have dropped them, chunks bitten out, ruined brown flesh oozing from puncture marks, the foot-tread texture that of a fresh dog turd. It's warm mangoes fresh from the tree, juice-sticky skin, overripe fruits frozen for iced daiquiris at sunset. The taste of papaya as it is meant to be, sweet, with the spoon-glide of butter. Rosella fruits harvested from wild sprigs, boiled into sweet—sour jam, or eaten straight, like tamarind fruit, until the tongue blisters and the mouth refuses.

A Darwinite favours the Wet to the Dry, when the heavens open, the tourists are few, festivals are over and the town slows its pace. This is Darwin time, when men surf waves forced by storm activity, all sand, thrash and dump. Kids scrape knees as they scoot boogie boards across sodden ovals. Rain might brew for days at a time, promising, with-holding, then – with thunderclaps as bugle – the monsoonal downpour. Heavy. Total. Hard as nails. Viewed from a distance, it assumes the innocent look of a flattened sheet of smoke. A storm can be so localised, it's like Nightcliff Pool's shadecloths: you drive through penetrating rain, wipers thrashing on the highest setting, into violent sunlight, as if the rain had never been. Within the storm, water angles from all directions, wind-pushed horizon-tally, diagonally, from the ground up, piercing like pearl spears arrowed in their thousands. Houses shudder and groan beneath thunder blasts heralded by strobes of lightning arcing so fast, commanding such sky–earth power, white light floods the space between ground and air, conjuring all shapes into sudden horizontal view.

Only frogs can soar above the sound of torrential rain on corrugated iron. Mottled brown marbled marsh frogs the size of mere dinner spoons reach over the thumping drumbeat with a high pitched 'kak, uk, kak'. The little males are loud but elusive. Seldom seen in the act, a successful night out sees a white foam concoction anchored to rock or vegetation, a delicate mousse of air bubbles and jelly floating atop water, cocooning their new eggs. Urging the rain along further, lime green tree frogs shake off their docile daytime manners to unleash the rock star vamps within. With heartbreaker eyes set on high alert, they leave their toilet bowls, vines and trees in search of downpipes and guttering to amp up the sound and get the party going. 'Burrrt, burrrt, burrrt', over and again – a noisy a cappella competition. Brief interludes, the next round even louder.

To be in Darwin is to worship the sinking sun, marking the fleeting band of lime green flashing the moment the dying star disappears, colouring the sky amber, crimson and mauve in its long wake. All social tensions disappear. This is the Darwin that is savoured, the Darwin that unites. It is the Darwin of fundamental things.

4

Future Darwin

Rebellion to sameness

Immediately after the South Australians signed the Northern Territory over to the Commonwealth Government, a new Administrator arrived, one John Anderson Gilruth. A Scotsman from Victoria, Gilruth had been a gifted veterinarian and academic, publishing papers on such practical topics as sheep maggots and worm nodules in Australian cattle. Cut with a patrician nose and assessing eyes, he had reconnoitred the north before his appointment and imagined its potential for mining, farming and pastoralism. As Administrator, he was pivotal to the establishment of the Vesteys Meatworks at Bullocky Point. He had used his skills as a fastidious civil servant to wear down Commonwealth dithering over the approvals required to establish Darwin's first major industrial development, a much-needed source of work and link to multinational industry. Yet, for all Gilruth's vision, there could not have been a worse choice for the small, mixed, troublesome northern settlement, nor worse timing.

Every year on 1 May, the international day of worker's rights, Darwinites commemorate their brief political insurgency, when unionists effectively deposed their Administrator, marching with an effigy and chanting about worker rights. Back on that fateful day, 17 December 1918, now known as the Darwin Rebellion, up to one thousand demonstrators marched to Government House, 'headed by a motor-car carrying a grotesque effigy of the Administrator tied to a stake'. The marchers had a demand: Gilruth the autocrat had to explain his five years of high-handed rule or leave his post. His face aching with fatigue, Gilruth eventually addressed the crowd. He avoided the little box the demonstrators had helpfully set up for him, choosing the symbolic security of the lawns of Government House, his voice lost to all but those pressed closest. As the crowd leant in to hear, the fence was people-crushed to the ground. Some dozen men advanced over the lawns as Gilruth fled the scene. He stayed in hiding for almost two months, nursing a sick daughter through fevers in terrible isolation, finally escaping under cover of darkness. It was 'an inglorious departure', writes Frank Alcorta. The family 'embarked on HMAS *Encounter*, a warship armed with eleven six-inch guns, sent in by the Federal Government in a theatrical and wholly unnecessary gesture to protect its representative'.

Like many senior public servants and politicians to follow, Gilruth liked the trappings of authority: the functions, chauffeurs and gardeners, the airy rooms with over-large tables and shimmering display cabinets. He considered his new posting a blank slate upon which he could imprint his authority. He found otherwise. For the workers, merchants, professionals, migrants and poly-ethnic families making up the human sinkhole that was old-time Darwin, Gilruth's autocratic ways were unbearable. When he slashed the wages of government field-survey hands and the Amalgamated Workers' Association went on strike to protest, Gilruth suppressed them brutally. He denied European workers any preferential contract treatment over the cheaper and less fractious Chinese. He placed the Top End's hotels under his administration in 1915 and controlled access to alcohol from thereon in, creating instant enemies of the town's many drinkers. He also made a powerful opponent in Harold Nelson, the trade union leader, and lost the respect of many of the town's key professionals.

Predictably, a Commonwealth inquiry later made the failings of Gilruth's administration almost exclusively a matter of personal style. 'Dr Gilruth', reviewer Ewing wrote, 'had little toleration for any person who disagreed with him, and was temperamentally unsuited for filling the office he occupied.' With Gilruth the convenient kicking boy, other contributing forces faded from view. Yet historians writing about the string of failed northern settlements and Darwin's unpromising early beginnings agree: governance was serially marred by short-term appointees with little connection to the place, the likelihood of well-oiled retirement elsewhere, scant finances to invest in public amenities, few ratepayers among the many absentee landlords, and limited powers to make decisions on issues of any true consequence.

When contemporary May Day marchers burn effigies in remembrance of the Darwin Rebellion, they are reminding crowds that worker rights remain in jeopardy. It raises the question: what else remains the same? Still new to governing as a political entity itself, the newly formed federal government acquired the Northern Territory just before World War I drained its coffers. Northern administration thus began as it would proceed, with a pattern of benign neglect and underinvestment interrupted by brash interventions. Refracted within the Territory fishbowl, the relatively small bits of the Commonwealth's policy expertise that get directed the Territory's way magnify locally out of proportion. It makes the Commonwealth's habit of intermittent attention feel like so much contempt and folly, when more accurately it is a matter of volatile issue-grab and hit-and-miss expertise.

For all that it chafes, the manacle is binding. The Territory was governed from the outside until the point of self-government in 1978. Even self-government is a regulatory courtesy, easily overturned. Expensive and extensive infrastructure needs for a small and transient population over a large land mass, the narrow, vulnerable bandwidth of economic outputs and deeply embedded radical poverty (aka 'Indigenous disadvantage') means ongoing reliance on federal funding. Being a mendicant economy might not suit the frontier image but it has made a good agar plate for culturing 'us and them' identities, incubated from the time of handover on.

Back in Gilruth's day, the national government treated the north as a distant colony. Local vexations were insignificant in the greater Commonwealth scheme. It took sustained agitation from the North Australian Workers Union, led by Gilruth's nemesis Harold Nelson, before the Territory was ceded a single, non-voting member of the House of Representatives in federal parliament. Swing forward to the 21st century and the NT government remains peripheral to most key negotiations. Without Commonwealth finances, the Northern Territory administration is little more than an engorged local government. Central control continues to be directed from Canberra regarding the overall allocation of the Northern Territory's budget, decisions about Defence spending, and – as importantly for the north – directions on Indigenous affairs. The NT does not get to decide which parcels of Crown land are earmarked for Defence purposes, what foreign power surveillance technologies will be hosted onshore, or even whether the place will become a special taxation zone.

Northern Territory legislative powers are flexed at Canberra's whim. Chief Minister Marshall Perron's voluntary euthanasia law was flicked away. Even the Northern Territory Emergency Response (commonly known as the Intervention) was out of Territory hands, although, as per common practice, the money earmarked to improve Indigenous circumstances was split among many beneficiaries. The influx of administrators from Canberra rivalled those that flooded the town during World War II. Money for public service positions in the service departments of housing, health, education and police took quantum leaps. Hotels charged premium rates for off-season stays. Hire cars were fully booked. Qantas put on a new flight that whipped suits from Canberra to Darwin on a Monday and got them back comfortably by Thursday night, with the Qantas Club functioning like Darwin Hotel's Green Room of old. A meeting place for likeminded, terribly important civil servants, consultants and journalists, each winnowing out the scraps of gossip and insider knowledge that passed for strategic intelligence during that intense policy flurry.

For all the continuities, the Territory puts a special stamp on its provincial politics. The politicians are known by name to their electors, most electorates are so small. And while they may be bit-players in terms of controlling the main revenues, they loom large in local preoccupations. The first party to be elected upon self-government, the Country Liberal Party, stayed in power for twenty-seven years, fighting Aboriginal land claims every step of the way. The land within town boundaries could not be claimed, forcing the local Larrakia to seek the Cox Peninsula across the harbour from Darwin. The CLP's response was swift. Darwin's town boundaries were extended by 4200 square kilometres to incorporate the Cox Peninsula too.

In the early years of self-government, when the

population was still small, the dirty deals seemed more brazen. Chief Minister Shane Stone took the opportunity granted by his concurrent roles as the First Law Officer and Attorney-General of the Northern Territory to appoint himself Queen's Counsel. When Labor's Clare Martin broke the decades-long CLP monopoly in 2001, more amusements followed. A departing political minder chose the Speaker's chair in Parliamentary Chambers to have sex with his girlfriend. Along with the tawdry antics, Labor also closely mimicked the CLP's formula for maintaining government: spend in the suburbs and whisk through development permits to keep cranes on the horizon and jackhammers in motion.

The August 2012 election returned the Country Liberal Party to government in its new guise as Indigenous flag-bearer, now boasting the largest number of Indigenous politicians ever elected to a state, territory or federal parliament in Australian history. With the swapping of Chief Minister Terry Mills for Adam Giles nine months in, the Northern Territory also became the first of Australia's self-governing states and territories to have an Indigenous leader. But Giles's ascent competed with other revolving door leadership issues in the same period: Victoria lost its premier the same week; there was yet another challenge to Prime Minister Julia Gillard; and Pope Benedict XVI became the first pope in 600 years to resign while still in office. It was a whimper rather than a bang of political distinction, somehow fitting in a place which, despite the pioneering attitude, is profoundly conservative.

It's the kind of contradiction Darwin is made of. It sits alongside another: for a place of such soul-grabbing natural beauty and staggering oppor-tunities for reinvention, Darwin is quite possibly the least beautifully designed of Australia's capital cities. And this too heralds a paradox, stemming as much from the strange kinds of good fortune that have come Darwin's way as its string of disasters.

There were five town plans created for Darwin between 1937 and 1950, and there have been uncountable others since. Some came close, but never close enough, to actually being implemented. The first of these imagined the CBD as a mili-tary base, an idea which suited the demands of the Royal Australian Navy. The navy might have had their way but for the new Administrator, Aubrey Abbott, a man more famous for viewing Aborigines as slave labour for the pastoral industry and his indecisive leadership during the Japanese bombings than for his aesthetic vision. Like Gilruth, Abbott was a stickler for etiquette and protocols in a place that melted both. But it was Abbott who looked at the foul sewers, broken roads and overcrowded dwellings of 1930s Darwin and imagined better. Convincing the Commonwealth to put up some funds, he had an experienced surveyor and planner, Ronald Alison McInnis, seconded from Queensland.

Arriving in September 1940, just as the Dry Season was ending, McInnis assessed the original grid that Goyder had laid down on the peninsula all those years ago. Dislodging gravel as he kicked at broken pavements, he took in the limited sewer works and saw a town still reliant on private wells, bores and household tanks. He lamented the large amount of prime land that was reserved for the military and rendered off-limits. From these haphazard pieces McInnis designed an extraordinary plan. He recommended more of the graceful elevated houses designed by tropical architect Beni Burnett; a widening of key thoroughfares; road sealing; modernising the sanitation; distinctive zoning for future residential, industrial and recreational areas; and removal of the civilian aerodrome from its then location in Parap. Consulting a botanist, he called for extensive planting of slow-growing trees, the kind that send down deep roots and survive without watering: poincianas, Mexican flame trees, banyans and figs.

Abbott loved the McInnis plan; the navy, not so much. Then war whacked such fripperies for six. From their perch as leaders of a garrison town, the military easily dictated how the place should be organised. They successfully urged the Commonwealth to compulsorily acquire all privately owned land in the Darwin area, which delayed the return of civilians well past the war's cessation and made everyone beggars for accommodation. They proffered an alternative plan for the town's rebuild, one which again made the CBD their own and parked civic administration elsewhere. To counteract these new threats, Abbott resecured McInnis's services, interrupting his imminent appointment to Tasmania.

Key issues had already been decided. War had 'municipalised' Darwin in a way peacetime had not. Military labour had finally sealed the Stuart Highway to Alice Springs, Darwin's arterial link with the rest of Australia. The Manton River had been impounded in 1942 to create Darwin's first water supply reservoir, allowing modern sewerage systems to be contemplated. Servicemen had systematically looted and destroyed shops and homes, so renovations were needed anyway. And the unsavoury shanties of old Chinatown had been blasted apart, courtesy of the Japanese. What the Japanese had not destroyed, the Commonwealth pushed over, determined Chinatown would never regenerate.

On this drastically wiped-clean drawing board, McInnis sketched a new plan. He imagined the entire area that the Navy had commandeered for itself – the area occupied today by Parliament House, the courts, the town hall ruins, Darwin city council offices and library – as a civic area surrounded by parkland. Looking at this area today, one might think McInnis succeeded. But in his vision, the precinct was not a collection of awkwardly sited buildings amid accidental bits of greenery and asphalt, as at present, but a grand symmetry, with pedestrian use at its heart. Additional green space would draw citizens together in an imagined park located between Smith and Cavenagh Streets. There was even the money to do it: £2 million promised by Prime Minister Curtin.

Clean slate, land acquisition and money: perfect ingredients for a City Beautiful.

Trouble was, McInnis's criticisms of the 'armed services demands for almost every prime piece of foreshore land for military purposes' won him few friends of influence. Canberra's response was typically distracted. Having spread responsibilities for northern administration across multiple portfolios, it created an interdepartmental committee – a recipe for indecision. Curtin had died. His successor Chifley had nation-building projects on his hands. Lacking any interest in expensive outlays in the foreign north, Prime Minister Robert Menzies was content to leave his longstanding Minister for Territories, Paul Hasluck, to take responsibility. Darwin's growth from the 1950s to the Cyclone came about through Hasluck's agitations. Tarred by his association with war-disgraced Administrator Abbott, McInnis was blamed for the Commonwealth's unpopular compulsory acquisition program and left the town to sort itself out.

Meantime, there were many new residents: gaunt-faced escapees from Europe desperate for new starts; war veterans piecing their lives back together as civilians; civilians as war's unacknowledged refugees. Some were young adventurers, moving to the north for excitement and courtship.

All arrived to an accommodation crisis, prolonged by squabbles over whose plan should be implemented and struggles with the Commonwealth over the paltry compensation offered for repossessed titles. Newcomers lived in the hot, corrugated iron Sidney Williams huts left over from service barracks in town, or bunked in hostels, strangers thrown together.

Their patience sorely tested, returning residents eventually took matters into their own hands, crafting shelters on blocks they felt were theirs with whatever came to hand. Some even grew fat on the post-war construction boom, snapping up Crown land as soon as it was released, privy to backroom feeds. Yet few looked at the scarred and ugly town as anything much in its own right. If anything, Darwin's dowdiness became something to be defended: 'If you don't like it,' redfaced men in singlets would growl from thickened tongues, 'go back to where you came from.' It took the audacity of men like Hans Vos, the developer behind the town's first purpose-built marina at Cullen Bay, to help prove the market value of the town's pockets of beauty.

Cyclone Tracy offered a new opportunity for starting afresh. Instead, the city stagnated, lacking the resources to attract new investment capital, or the capital to renovate its own resources. 'Tracy Trauma' fortress homes, cement walls with wind-out caravan-sized windows that trapped the heat, were constructed in the new suburbs of Wanguri, Anula and Wulagi. Hippies trekking across Asia trickled through, but tourist facilities were grim, offering out-of-date and expensive options that soon wore thin. The many surviving Burnett houses from Parap and Larrakeyah were stacked onto trucks and freighted to rural blocks, while out-of-fashion fittings – burnt-orange Formica, lime green upholstery material and brown plastic tapware – were offloaded from enterprising southern businesses onto desperate consumers at vastly inflated prices. It was a time of consultants living in demountable huts, cashing in on the disaster, and bureaucracy gone mad.

The Darwin Reconstruction Commission, with its 'three token locals', as town planner Graham Bailey puts it to me, came up with some good ideas amid the mayhem. They wanted to relocate the airport; improve the roads and make them amenable to public transport; close streets and create quiet cul-de-sacs; acquire homes from surge areas and make these non-residential. To improve noise screening and to prevent the clash of driveways with arterial traffic, each major road was to have a buffer zone either side, planted with trees and laced with footpaths. But only $1 million was set aside for the compulsory acquisitions needed to realise these ideas — enough to buy a handful of the 500 lots estimated.

Meantime, people caught in the buffer zones were neither allowed to rebuild nor able to be rec-ompensed. Building costs ratcheted up as assorted administrators, advised by phalanxes of external consultancy firms, went into coding overdrive. They demanded corrugated roofs be bolted along every single flute for the first two lines and that each house have its own cyclone shelter. Concrete thicknesses jumped in width and depth, using wire mesh set at gauges strong enough for an industrial site. The tie-down bolts from the floor to the roof doubled in diameter and tripled in price. All of it was untested, a coding born of guesswork, paper-work and profiteering. Locals struggling with mortgage repayments, insurance schemes that paid original capital values but stopped shy of replace-ment costs, and no banks willing to loan money on such uncertain tenure conditions, lost money, went bankrupt, left town for good or ground their teeth and set up tents and caravans underneath exposed floorboards.

As often happens at key times in Territory history, the federal government was preoccupied with its own money troubles. The Whitlam administration was resorting to shady backroom deals to borrow money to pay its debts; supply was blocked; the Governor-General stepped in; Australia got a new government. Malcolm Fraser solved the housing and reconstruction crises of the north by passing the buck entirely. The Commonwealth established a fully elected Northern Territory Legislative Assembly, then self-government. The rebelliousness that had once demanded political representation was now protesting self-government. Public servants were worried the shift to becoming Northern Territory administrators would reduce their generous hazard allowances and make them permanent residents. While the Larrakia were staging sit-down protests to fight for their land, public servants went on strike when departments were amalgamated or subsidised airfares were reduced.

Each successive Chief Minister since self-government has introduced a plan for the city and region, few with McInnis's passion. There's an abundance of forgettable documents sharing an earnest, humourless narrative structure: *Planning for Growth, Foundations for the Future, Transforming the Territory, Territory 2030*, and now *Framing the Future*. All mention the need to release land for development by fast-tracking approvals, proclaiming over and again the Northern Territory's enormous potential, how it will thrive because of its minerals, cattle, multiculturalism, advantageous location and – most deluding of all claims – its pristine environment. None foresee a way around ongoing dependency on the Commonwealth. None give the prognosis of rising sea levels, temperatures hovering around 40 degrees Celsius for most of the year and more extreme 'weather events', or strategies for climate-proofing the city, any prominence. None discuss what being at the pointy end of military preparedness implies for civilians. The absence of detailed local plans for Darwin's sustainability is mirrored by optimistic national ideas about charging the north with salvaging Australia's future. There is new/old talk of making the north the food bowl and water tap for a desiccating Australia, and of creating tax breaks for companies who headquarter here. Both ideas have been tried before but, who knows, fifty-first time lucky?

The boosterism ignores history in many ways. With the exception of Palmerston's collaboration with mosquito managers, the transformation of post-cyclone Darwin had little to do with Territory politics or planning and everything to do with American military strategy, the least acknowledged city architect of all.

Carceral city

It is entirely possible to experience Darwin as something of a pleasure dome, a world of genteel evasions and married midriffs. On balmy tropical evenings in the Dry Season, the town lights up with creative festivals, racing carnivals and galas. There are award-winning restaurants and yacht voyages offering champagne by sunset, hipster jewellery and flowing silks at the bohemian events, plunging necklines and upswept hairstyles where the more expensive alcohol flows.

To explore the Darwin that is unknown to any tourist, I opt instead for a bird's-eye view from an ultralight aircraft. The small band of pilots of these frail-looking craft keep their machines at a small field at Noonamah, down the Stuart Highway, past Darwin's industrial estates and near the first of the region's crocodile farms. As we puttered down the airfield, leaving early to avoid the turbulent thermals, wallabies bounded past and wood pigeons piped a farewell refrain. An ultralight flies low and slow, revealing a perspective that hill-less Darwin otherwise cannot offer. A thousand feet up and the tough, delicate topography of Darwin comes into view, a place of military zones, industrial sites and back-to-the-future incarceration compounds. There is the huge chunk of habitable land consumed by the airport; the mangroves as they hold the slow-drowning delta system in fragile check; the inlets of East and West Arm, showing how close to inundation Darwin's harbour has become. Between the deltas, on slightly higher land, 5-acre rural blocks and allotments scraped over for their gravel and sand. Extractive sites are everywhere, some current, some abandoned – miniature versions of their bigger cousins, the open pit mines. Old quarries are filled with water, sluice pits of unnatural pink or milky green.

It is not just the gravel diggers who have scraped and levelled. There are raw earth patches and building works in all directions. My pilot points out the new detention centre, a skinny village of metal demountables stacked one on top of the other, 1500 rooms with two people apiece. This is the Wickham Point Development, destined to be Australia's largest on-land immigration detention centre. The Paspaley family is a majority shareholder, farming people instead of pearls. They join another money-maker, 'Foxy' Robinson, for whom public hostility to asylum seekers is a more practical affair of financial opportunity. One of Foxy's compounds stands to the left of the entrance road to Darwin airport. A series of navy blue demountables stacked one atop another, joined by stairs and narrow balconies, they can easily be converted into temporary accommodation for 'fly-in, fly-out' (FIFO) workers by removing the barbed wire fencing and calling it a hotel.

The new immigration detention centre sits astride old prawn farms, shallow rectangles of dirty salt water framed by mud embankments, the abandoned farming ideas of earlier times. It is being built at a site refused by the Japanese flagship oil and gas extraction corporation Inpex as too cruel for its future FIFO workers, being so breathless and full of biting insects.

We fly over another site, this one the new prison complex, being built to cope with the Territory's burgeoning prison population. The building carapaces are in a circle divided into sections — like an orange that's been halved then had three segments at a time pulled away from the pith — occupied by an inner ringlet of watchtowers. It is a perfect Benthamite 'panopticon': an apparatus of social discipline made famous by philosopher Michel Foucault. Jailing people (like assaulting people, rolling cars or drinking a lot) is something the Northern Territory does exceptionally well. The signs of trauma are everywhere: little plastic flower shrines fixed to electricity poles and road signs, sun-faded and dusty; a makeshift cross with felt-pen hatchings saying a loved one died right here. And in the jails, different kinds of human wreckage. Nationally in 2013, reports the Australian Bureau of Statistics, the average daily imprisonment rate was 172 prisoners per 100 000 adult population. The Northern Territory: 889 prisoners per 100 000, more than four times the Australian average. There's no mistaking the racial character of the prisoner population either. Eighty per cent of adult prisoners are Indigenous, a slight improvement on Darwin's juvenile detention centre, where less than 10 per cent of the teenage inmates are *not* Indigenous. One more thing can be added to Darwin's list of firsts: it can also boast Australia's highest rates of homelessness.

As we zoom over the Howard Springs region, an even more barren site appears, this one lined by rows of single-storey demountables, densely packed together in regimented blocks, only metres apart.

'What's that?' I yell into the helmet mike, over the drone of the aircraft engine at my back.

'That's the new village for workers for the Inpex gas plant,' the pilot shouts back. 'Locals keep suggesting it should be turned into an old people's home after they're finished with it.'

Whoever suggests this obviously hasn't taken a close look at what they're talking about, I muse. Perhaps they've taken the cute term 'accommodation village' to imagine something more salubrious than the Lego-land fortress of asphalt, dongas, kitchen block, tavern and dining halls below me. It has been designed so that Inpex workers will be kept to a tight schedule, following a Japanese Fordist model that echoes the organised tent city that lined Port Darwin in the early decades of settlement, when Goyder frogmarched his work squadrons to map and subdivide 270 000 hectares of strange land in nine months flat. In future times the Inpex Accommodation Village will be greened with instant lawns and transplanted trees. It will have a cricket pitch, swimming pool and basketball courts. An onsite medical centre is up and running, together with a cinema complex. There is a bus depot too, to transport workers to and from the processing centre, to and from the airport, to and from the town; no need to clog the roads with the expected 3500 FIFO workers. The Inpex workers are meant to arrive, work, depart. The facilities will ensure that their like or dislike of Darwin itself will be of no real consequence, even as their presence helps price-gouge the real estate market.

The plan is to suck the gas and condensates from the Ichthys gas field off the Kimberley coastline in Western Australia – forty years' worth, they say – and squeeze what cannot be immediately processed along the longest subsea pipeline in the southern hemisphere, nearly 900 kilometres' worth, all the way to Darwin. There, at a facility called Blaydin Point (better known to locals as the Middle Arm Peninsula), the gas will be cooled to below minus 161 degrees Celsius, a process which requires enormous energy inputs, even outside the tropics. Thus compressed into liquefied natural gas (LNG), it will be shipped in tankers to Japan and re-gasified, supplying more than 10 per cent of Japan's gas imports. Sucked, squeezed, shipped: does this make it like the fishing industry? From the Greek word for fish, 'ichthys' also names the two curved strokes that outline the shape of a fish in Christian symbolism. Perhaps the metaphor takes us from Jesus, the giver of fish, to Japan, the taker of gas, via Darwin, the eager disciple.

Ichthys is the largest private capital investment in Australian history – a coup for the Territory, which won the decision over rival Western Australia by not demanding that some of the gas be reserved for domestic consumption. Onshore processing in Western Australia invokes a 15 per cent domestic gas reservation policy for domestic purchasers (including local industries). Technically, the gas isn't owned by the Territory, so reserving any would require paying royalties to Western Australia via the Commonwealth, as the Territory's financial patron, and there is no word on that either. At any rate, the next fifteen years' worth of LNG production has already been sold to overseas buyers. Instead, as locals protest the continual dredging of the harbour and destruction of recreational fishing zones, vast economic benefits are promised to outweigh any drawbacks.

Looking down from the sky, the future of the city hails its past. Habits of incarceration are buried deep in Darwin's bones, from the earliest days of settlement, when compounds were filled with immigrant–Aboriginal progeny and jails spilt over with the unwanted, to now, where new reservations for brown-skinned asylum seekers and worker enclaves are being erected at speed and the jail is quadrupled in size.

We see a cluster of satellite domes like a toadstool forest dotting the shoreline at Shoal Bay, inaccessible. We are not allowed to fly over those. The route we fly is hedged in by invisible fences, blocking massive grids from trespass, difficult to see but as real as barred gates with sentry guards. The divided sky mimics Darwin's lesser-known status as a garrison town: there but not there, known but not known, remembered then forgotten.

Mango orchards and market gardens interrupt the military–industrial complexes. Buckley Road in Darwin's Humpty Doo is known to horticulturists as Little Vietnam. A mango business goes by the name of Saigon Farm. A patchwork emerges. Fields of bok choy, dragon fruit, bitter melon, snake and winged beans open beneath us, the hard-earned results of Vietnamese farmers pulling food from this tough land. These boat people had arrived in vessels held together by hope and despair, to a country which, back then, had welcomed them. They transformed Darwin into a place where multiculturalism is consumed by tourists and locals alike, in pork ball satays with their halo of garlic fumes; fresh-caught mud crabs, still live and vengeful, hoping to wrest a claw free of the plastic ties holding them prisoner in styrofoam boxes; pho soup broth simmering in giant pots, ready to be ladled onto bowls of rice noodle; and soft rice paper rolls spiced with chilli, crushed peanut and fragrant mints. Funny how the fall of Saigon to the Vietnam People's Army in 1975 led to this: a Vietnamese refugee resettlement program that utterly changed the town. Exotic ginger species and other ornamental plants transformed gardens while Vietnamese horticulture made the markets the tourist paradise they are today.

We pass over the new housing estates being built in Palmerston for people getting a foothold in the expensive real estate market. The besser block constructions push to their boundaries. Between fence and house there's room only for air-conditioning units, a neighbourhood of machines permanently exchanging hot-air gossip. Without air-conditioning, these houses would be unliveable for large chunks of the year. It is the despair of local architects, who lament the lack of environmental design. Yet the boxed panorama below represents the desires of the sojourning majority, and what the majority demands, the market supplies. It has got to the point where the highest energy efficiency ratings are awarded to houses that reduce airflow and insulate for air-conditioning. It is an energy efficiency system which penalises louvres in favour of small, double-glazed sliding windows and thick cement walls.

Over to our north-west from the skies of Palmerston we can see the spiked high-rises of Darwin's CBD. Glimmerglass office towers and accommodation complexes sprout where the town's former low-density housing and oil tanks used to be. The city does not embrace its ocean necklace but turns its buildings inward and skyward, rewarding the well-heeled with the cooling effects of air-conditioning, hotel pools, turquoise views and underground carparks. Only one stretch of waterfront is permanently reserved for public use in the CBD — the Esplanade, a narrow strip of green that miraculously survived from the days of Goyder's surveys on.

New Darwin represents the bonanza and cataclysm that is the dazzling Inpex/military build-up. Whole buildings in the many new high-rise complexes in and around the old peninsula are filled with strangers, non-resident workers the fastest-growing demographic. Speculative pricing and negatively geared investors have made Darwin's real estate market a rival to Sydney's. Those with the cash to purchase have watched their accounts grow fat. For others, the skyrocketing prices weigh their futures down. Darwin offers work, but not the hope of a home, the toll price for living in a boomtown. It has become a prosperous, unequal city. The town's repeat failure to plan infrastructure around future residential needs is biting back with a vengeance: old sewerage systems are choking under the load; new run-offs create swamps in built-in residential zones; a third dam is needed; the electricity network generates higher pricing to pay for upgrades after years of neglect.

Some locals eye off the hunk of higher land sitting in Darwin's belly, decorated by languorous airstrips able to handle the heavy, slow-launching B52 bombers, and imagine this above-sea-level and centrally located land being opened for residential development. There are no military planes on the tarmac when I go to meet the Commanding Officer of 13 Squadron at Darwin's RAAF base: the Dry Season exercises have been over for some weeks. It adds to the sense of availability. The red-haired CO greets me in full blues, gold buttons gleaming, for the Governor-General will be visiting later that day. We meet in vintage RAAF headquarters next to the runway, an austere fibreboard building from the 1930s, when extravagant ceiling heights compensated for constricted horizontal space.

Of his twenty-three years in the RAAF, thirteen have been spent in and out of Darwin. His perspective takes in other places – Somalia, Afghanistan – but his enthusiasm for this, the largest runway and most capable airfield the RAAF operates in Australia, has not lessened a jot. He knows every inch of this airfield, from the decaying pipes underneath to where the ordnances are stockpiled. When he first came to Darwin, the barracks and airfield were on the outskirts of town. Today, residential and light industrial estates nibble like rats on all sides.

He reminds me that there has been a RAAF

presence in Darwin since the 1940s, and that they have always enjoyed warm community acceptance, albeit more people might complain now about the noise of fighter jets taking off for their practice manoeuvres every June. I nod, knowing how our whole house shakes and talk is stopped as the air explodes with jet fighter noise. They set off in relays, so close you can train binoculars onto the wings and name the craft – heaven for plane-spotters. We agree it is unusual to have an inter-national airfield and military base smack in the middle of a capital city, but when I ask whether the airfield will ever be made available for resi-dential development, he shakes his head, chuckling sympathetically.

'The airport here is highly capable, with a large runway able to support just about any aircraft ever built.'

Shifting the airfield would be untenable in his opinion, costing billions of dollars and adding at least an hour's drive at either end of travel times. It is the military purpose that gives this small town its high-end airfield in the first place – a reminder, if one was needed, of how deeply entwined Dar-win's existence is with that of national defence.

Pin in the map

It had started as a normal enough night, over a decade ago now. A fifteen year old has gone to Mindil Beach markets with her friends, an attractive, open-hearted, vibrant group of Darwin girls. As they wait for a taxi home, two charming US Marines ask to share their cab and, even better on this warm night, offer the use of their hotel pool.

I hold my breath against the dread creeping through my gut as the mother retells this story, knowing how moral judgements, like demons, are already stalking a tight circle around how it might unfold. Darwin is a place, after all, that registered the highest sexual assault rates against women in this country the last time comparative national data was ever collected. Per capita, we throw back alcohol – the key trigger in assaults – thrice as much as our national counterparts too, and that's without Indigenous consumption mixed into the count.

The girls should be at home already. They are too young to be out drinking. When has going to hotels with strangers ever been a wise thing to do? But they were not thinking about anything but cute heroes, the kind that save nice white girls, not hurt them. The US Marines are gentlemen with exquisite manners. They open car doors and say 'ma'am' like no Darwin bloke even knows how to. Locals have long been told to welcome visiting servicemen and women, for their important benefits to the economy and national security.

An odourless additive in a pink drink traps the two girls in a garish paralysis. When they return to consciousness, men are pushing into them, with more standing in line. Hours later, they sit naked at a round table, the functional kind found in administrative offices as well as hotel rooms. Before they can get their clothes back or be released from their imprisonment, they are videotaped, saying to each man in turn, 'I was not raped. I wanted this.'

The mother knows teenagers are notoriously hard work, but she just hadn't expected such an abrupt personality change in her oldest child. From considerate and pleasant to surly and unpredictable. For a couple of months now, her daughter shouts instead of talking. Nothing brings a smile. Telling me now about her blind interventions then, the mother claw-fights her tears, swallowing as her larynx constricts. I keep writing, eyes down, at war with my throat too. Perhaps a festive gathering would work some magic, the mother had thought. A Cyclone Tracy survivor, suppressing the stiffening dread that Christmas storm clouds always bring, she created a family feast. She carefully dressed their round table, maternal love flooding each nudge of cutlery, napkin and plate.

Seeing the glorious tribute, her daughter grows more monstrous. She screams. She runs. She goes missing for days.

For the police, the Christmas/New Year period is mayhem on the roads and in houses — drunken crashes and domestic violence, one after the other. Teenagers run away all the time. The girl is fifteen, partying somewhere with her mates, most like, like Darwin kids always do this time of year. It takes a mother-hunt to track her down.

After months of shouted rages, her daughter cannot speak her story. But she can write on little slips of paper, one glass-shard at a time, about the day two months before when representatives of the military–industrial geopolitical world invaded her innermost world and broke it apart. There had been no doctor, no police, no blood tests, no rape kit: just private shame and a deep conviction it was all her fault. She had felt like there was no place to go so she bottled it up, exploding erratically at the one person who would keep on loving her no matter what.

Over a decade later, in November 2011, both mother and daughter watched as the first black US President, Barak Obama, stood with the first female Australian Prime Minister, Julia Gillard, to announce the permanent rotation of up to 2500 US Marines per year through Darwin Defence facilities. Not surprisingly, they did not share the community celebrations of this historic occasion but joined the tiny crowd of protesters instead.

'Just tell me this, Tess, tell me — how did an American invasion happen with no consultation with the Australian people? Why are we told to see it all as positive and not ask any critical questions?'

Theories crowd my mind, yet I feel gagged too. 'That which brings money to Darwin buys easy community approval,' I go to say, but feel such glib words are as useless as those of men with flash epaulettes describing global military strategy. I want to take her question seriously. Why are these momentous changes of so little interest to the wider Australian public? As Professor Harry Gelber recently noted, commenting on Australia's fast-changing geopolitical and geostrategic position, 'Few of the policy issues facing Australia are more important, yet have received less public attention. Even the government seems only half aware of the looming changes.' My search for answers sets me tracking between the larger world of Australian foreign policy and the smaller one of Territory settlement history.

One thread leads back to World War II, when Australians finally came to grips with the hopelessness of relying on British naval supremacy as a national defence posture and firmed an alternative alliance with the United States. Tagging along with a new English-speaking big brother also bred complacency. Post-war Defence spending in Australia had fallen to a pittance when, facing looming defeat in Vietnam, the US military reassessed how it would maintain its worldwide military dominance without going bankrupt. Getting its allies to pick up some of their tab was part of the solution. President Nixon raised the threshold for US intervention in Allied defence to all-out nuclear attack. Henceforth, the Nixon doctrine asserted,

US allies like Australia should be more self-reliant. Or, at least, should have a force structure whose arsenal and communications systems permit inter-operability with the United States (after all, self-reliance was never meant to mean self-sufficiency). To put all this differently, Australia's defence posture is one of strategic dependence, within and by means of the ANZUS alliance. And in allying with America, Australia also purchases US weaponry and equipment, dressed in arguments about the importance of joint deployments and mutually beneficial trade.

The shift to a more intensively trained, smaller and more expensively equipped Australian Defence Force brought with it a need for large spaces to practice with long-range gear — just the sort of asset under Commonwealth control in the north of Australia. Otherwise, it would be like buying computer techware powerful enough to create and edit high-fidelity multimedia productions while knowing only how to use the word-processing function. Meantime, Canberra think tanks identified northern Australia as the most likely location for direct threats. With its deep-sea shipping access, military airfield, all-weather highway and large-scale freighting facilities, the port of Darwin was also the only place 'from which Australia could project an assertive role northwards' in protecting the passage between the Indian and Pacific Oceans via the South China Sea and through the Indonesian archipelago. But with most of Australia's Defence personnel sitting in the southern states, deploying to the north would be a cumbersome affair. It took 'the aircraft carrier HMAS *Melbourne* five days steaming at best speed from Sydney to bring urgently required aid to Darwin in the aftermath of Cyclone Tracy'. Thus began the reorientation of Australia's defence to the north, creating the biggest Defence electorate in Australia and one of the largest single real-estate holders in the Territory.

The Army Presence in the North (APIN) project rescued Darwin from the 1990 Australia-wide recession and reversed its population plunge. There was an influx of close to 3000 personnel, 500 support vehicles and 200 armoured fighting vehicles (Leopard tanks, eight-wheeled amphibious armoured vehicles, M113 armoured personnel carriers, which had proved their versatility in pushing through jungle thickets in Vietnam), and with each decision the Defence defibrillator sent an electric pulse into the town's economic heart. Robertson Barracks was purpose-built at Palmerston to accommodate one of the Australian Army's two regular brigades, a boon for Darwin's languishing construction industry. Land was requisitioned for weapons ranges, including the Bradshaw Field Training Area, near Timber Creek, south-west of Darwin.

The widespread community approval of Defence initiatives has unacknowledged roots in these lands too. The silence on Darwin's new/old identity as a garrison town is aided and abetted by the property legacies of dispossession, the colonial vestiges that are seldom connected to present-day opportunities, least of all when describing what US extraterritorial bases might be drawing upon.

Bradshaw was a former cattle station in the Victoria River Downs region. It had first been commandeered in 1894 by Captain Joseph Bradshaw, back when 'the country was wild and the blacks a continual source of trouble and danger'. Two decades later, as he lay dying of gangrene in Darwin hospital after an operation had turned septic, Joseph's only wish was that he be buried back at the station 'under a cairn of stones on one of the rugged mountain peaks', next to his brother Fred, who'd been 'murdered by blacks some years

ago'. Lands claimed for cattle in Australia's forgotten inland wars were ideal training grounds for
Allied wars offshore. There was always water, a
vital resource, and since leftover Aboriginal lands
had been neglected for years, and cattle stations
had big runs and scarce else, a cheque could buy
large slabs of country with little civilian infrastructure to be demolished or disputed. When the
army acquired Bradshaw in 1996, it secured nearly
800 000 hectares, just shy of Cyprus in size,
together with another 200 000 hectares from the
acquisition of the Delamere Air Weapons Range,
south of Katherine, and 100 000 hectares at the
Mount Bundey Military Training Area, south of
Darwin. These three areas make up the North
Australian Range Complex, one of the largest
military training areas in the world.

But it is the northern sky which is the crown
jewel in Australia's Defence treasure pile. In terms
of area and volume, it is larger than anywhere else
on the planet, without the traffic or curfews more
common to first-world facilities.

'The volume of airspace we use for a Pitch
Black exercise is larger than a lot of European
countries,' a RAAF expert told me. 'You're talking
about an airspace volume that is almost half the

size of Great Britain. Most countries just don't have an airspace availability like that.'

It is not just the airspace, but what goes with it.

'To have this volume of airspace, and airfields capable of supporting large numbers of aircraft, and then air weapons ranges associated with them as well – the air weapons ranges at Delamere and now out at Bradshaw – it just makes for a phenomenal training opportunity. Add to that, six months of the year you can be guaranteed perfect weather for your exercise.'

Such real estate and air combat assets caught the eye of US military strategists as they recalculated their Asia–Pacific presence, and Australia has been generous in its sharing. The surprise announcement made in Darwin, in 2011, with Obama cheered by units of professional fighters and Gillard smiling by his side, is no small affair. With the rotation of Marines comes greater overall access to Australian bases and airfields, increasing use of naval facilities, and the ability to take fuel, ammunition and spare parts in any live action.

The girl's mother knows all this. Without the personal scarring, she may even have joined the majority in thinking the positives outweigh any negatives. She accepts the Marine Corps are a *fait accompli*, that locals can't veto this kind of thing. Perhaps Australia itself has no choice. It is so hard to know where the power to shape truly consequential policy lies these days. Would there be trade embargoes if we sought to make our own alliances in the region, without American approval? Would America be content to leave the world's largest uranium deposits alone?

No matter. She asks only that the Marines stay on their ships or in the barracks, and that the Status of Forces Agreement (SOFA) is reviewed. Under SOFA, first signed in 1963 and unchanged since, if US personnel commit an offence under Australian law while in the course of their duties, Australian law will apply – unless a decision is made to hand over to US jurisdiction. But when it came to getting local Darwin police to investigate the girls' gang rape in Darwin, the detectives flailed, not knowing whose authority held sway. The mother reined in her frustration and pushed further, but her questions to police, the US Embassy, the Attorney-General's Department,

went without response, until journalist Paul
Toohey exposed Australia's ambivalent response to
this and other US military sexual assaults in *The
Australian*. Still, the case never went to trial. The
prosecution said it would be like being raped all
over again, and recommended against proceeding.

The Australians associated with Defence that I
have talked to, officially and unofficially, are far
from brutish. I sense they, and most likely the
visiting Marines, highly trained ambassadors all,
would view violent crimes against civilians with
horror and revulsion. These are men and women
who serve their countries, not harm them. Intelligent, humorous and knowledgeable, the Defence
viewpoint goes well beyond Darwin's near cata-
tonic indifference to world affairs. Personnel talk
matter-of-factly about Darwin as a pin in the map,
a node in a wider techno-strategic field, one which
relates to Timor, Papua New Guinea, the Solomon
Islands, Fiji, Indonesia, Vietnam, Cambodia,
Japan, Korea, China, Iraq, Iran, Afghanistan, Ant-
arctica, the United States, the Balkans.

Seeing through Defence eyes, I learn how in

military exercises Darwin is not really Darwin, but morphs into other places: south-east Asian villages sheltering adversaries in hidden basements; a middle-eastern stronghold; a desert with terrorists armed with lethal chemical weapons; a hostile sky filled with enemy craft. In training, they practise how to view the world from the thickened windows of armoured vehicles; how to engage enemies from behind cement walls; how to deal with the heat of combat in the sweat of the tropics; how to detect and intercept the enemy within a blinding field of blue skies and high clouds. Much as the local newspaper reports visiting forces in trivialising terms – 'Marines Come Ashore to Share Their Toys' – the make-believe has a deadly intent.

The resources needed to do all that is asked of Defence must be as long as a piece of string but, beyond exalting our troops, it seems not to be a conversation the community is prepared to have. With all the budget cuts, I learn there's much that risks being neglected, from anti-piracy work and protection of Australia's marine territories to development of closer ties with other allies, India and China included. Some lament the fatigue being carried in the bodies of naval personnel as they are flogged to stay on duty for longer and longer periods, doing the political work of asylum seeker repulsion as part of Operation Resolute, on ships that are falling apart. Their flesh registers chemical stress markers at levels equal to those triggered by immersion in live combat – one of the many hidden costs of border protection.

Just as there is dangerously little decompression time for the navy, Darwin is also renowned for its high-tempo operations across the forces. One man I meet, ex-Defence, tells me he wears his heart on his sleeve, but I sense sorrow, too, in the way his face crumples along weary lines, between an otherwise upbeat account of life in the ADF. His still-young son is already a veteran of two wars, a fact he views with 'a mixture of horror, pride and worry'. New to Darwin, he is astonished that locals do not seem to understand they are in the thick of military action, noting that Australia has been continually at war since going to action in Timor in 1998.

I am astonished in turn. For all my concern to see Darwin through a military lens, I was not conscious of the country's ongoing warfare before this chilling reminder. Yet I *do* know Darwin as a military town. After the cyclone, I was evacuated in a military plane to an army base. I remember how different it felt in Darwin, when folk in Sydney and Melbourne marched to support East Timor's fight for independence, almost a cerebral affair, while tanks rolled down our main streets, the khaki-green metal dappled by the silvery hues of dawn. Military aircraft roared overhead and men in United Nations fatigues stood in line for their milk at local grocery stores.

Despite the relentless budget tightening, every effort is made to make the high-tempo north bearable for single 'uniforms' and those with families, from Defence liaison officers in schools to an increasing array of accommodation choices. The Defence Community Organisation (DCO) headquarters in Darwin are part of a national network of support services available to help families 'make the most of the challenges and opportunities provided by the military way of life'. Together with the Veterans and Veterans Families Counselling Service, they provide courses on pain management; advice on how to help a friend with suicidal thoughts, sleep strategies, disciplining children without yelling or hitting, and doing anger differently; guidance on community resources for families — finding a vet, how local council works, how to beat the heat. A comprehensive menu for coping with military life before, during and after deployments. Some love the lifestyle, the camping, fishing and hunting opportunities; others count sleeps until their next rotation, insulating themselves from the tropical environment with trips to the Golden Mile on Mitchell Street and retreats to flat-screen televisions, video games and the cool blessing of air-con.

A poster at the DCO front counter sends a thrill up my spine. It shows a grim-faced modern digger carrying a child, flop-armed and brown-skinned, saved from an unnamed fiery catastrophe in the background. It is the kind of heroic image used in recruitment drives or in political explanations of the latest American build-up: greater preparedness for humanitarian aid and disaster relief operations. The newly built Darwin Military Museum at East Point provides the next most common rationale: a narrative of blood debt. In one viewing room, animated planes hurtle at the viewer from a high screen, as if from the sky. The Japanese planes are light, fast, manoeuvrable, coming one after another, machine guns spraying bullets across the ground, bombs falling like long stitches zippering the sky, loud sounds of gunfire and explosions, leavened with voiceovers from survivors who recovered the dead and wounded.

As in military museums across Australia, the race wars of settlement are not mentioned. And the American War in Vietnam is a passive exhibit in a disused bunker. The key museum message concerns the special military relationship enjoyed by Australians and Americans. Nearly half the men who died on the first day of the Japanese air raids on Darwin were American. American forces stayed on and fought the marauding attacks over the next two years to hold Australian ground, many lying dead in unmarked graves. Having Darwin become a US 'lily-pad' (a base that is not a base, but a smaller, 'cooperative security location') is simply an extension of an old and honourable alliance.

Not so, say BaseWatch, a local activist group determined to keep an eye on the American garrisons encircling the planet and now Darwin, who follow America's global realignment of bases and troops under their 'Asia pivot' with increasing wariness. Intrigued, I arrange to meet with Base-Watch members at a kebab shop next to a service station in Malak. It is noisy and out of the way, which somehow suits the obscurity of our topic.

One of the BaseWatch members who agrees to meet me is also ex-Defence, concerned that today's 'lily-pad' is tomorrow's behemoth, and naught to do with Australian self-reliance. 'American Marines are trained killers', I am told, over messy bites of kebab. The US will be hopping across their network of lily-pads like frogs toward prey. To BaseWatch members, it is more patriotic, not less, to probe the implications of Australia's enduring subservience to US military power in terms of our relationship with China, a topic equally close to Darwin's historical heart. Darwinites have a responsibility to be more aware of the national implications of what is happening here, they insist, wryly acknowledging they are near-alone with their questions.

Newly sensitised after my meetings with citizens, former and current military, I note the insistent positivity of official news releases. There's little on the naval fatigue, still less on what a proper spend for Australia's future security might need to be, and next to nothing on the potential civilian risks of being a pin in the map — a concern that is dismissed as unrealistic whenever it is raised. There are two government-commissioned consultancy reports on the anticipated social impact of the US Marine Corps rotations list that mostly negate its identified risks.

Inevitably, most Territory politicians talk up the economic benefits and suppress anything messier. While they are not in charge of the decisions, they have a key role to play in massaging the message. Addressing a recent seminar hosted by Charles Darwin University, Deputy Chief Minister David Tollner outlined a future where, adding to the dollars spent during exercises, large sheds could profitably be built by locals to house excess military hardware 'beyond the wire'. Perhaps this odd benefit was the only safe thing he could list, given his strenuous avoidance of the bonanza already underway in Darwin's fleshpot industry.

The local media do not share the Minister's coyness but gleefully report on the safely salacious, telling readers that 'Darwin's prostitutes and local ladies have been busy trying to keep pace with the swell of cute, horny US seamen on our shores.'

According to this article, when the USS *Peleliu* and USS *Pearl Harbor* docked in Darwin a few years ago, Darwin surged with a new libidinal energy as the ships 'unleashed hundreds of young, well-cut and hot-to-trot sailors ... Ship rules mean no sex on board – beyond what's on offer in a magazine,' reports the journalist, before citing an escort agency operator, Michelle Love, describing the positive impact on her business. Ms Love says 'her 30 girls had been kept busy servicing the Yankees' and that 'the US boys were never any problem. "They treat the girls like gold."'

The 'only possible issue was competition from the amateurs', the journalist continues, concluding with Ms Love's main complaint: '"Every horny woman comes out of the woodwork," she said. "But there's enough to go around."'

Brothels are not legal in the Northern Territory, but prostitution is. Licensed escort agencies can arrange visits from sex workers twenty-four hours a day, seven days a week, to your home or motel room, rented by the hour, choice of Australian, Asian or European, cup size, age range. Another player has entered the scene with Darwin's mining/construction/Defence boom: the Chinese massage parlour. Competitors to the escort agencies, they have been undercutting prices and providing services onsite, yet elude police detection.

Too scared to try myself, I had male friends tell me how Darwin's flourishing 'rub-and-tug' scenario works.

'You go in and they ask you something like, "How's your day?" and you reply, "Oh, not so good. I need a good cheering up." And unless you ask for a "happy ending", they'll presume you're there for a bone fide massage. You pay by leaving a "tip".'

'You just sit to one side and watch the kind of men who go in,' another woman tells me, snorting derisively as she pulls in another lungful of ciga-rette smoke. 'There's no mystery. They're not going in for the whale music, you know.'

Could it be that brothels that are not brothels and bases that are not bases go together, matching the way Darwin's status as a high-end military site is also hidden in full view? It is like the clear skies of the Dry Season, our bewitching tropical winter. Looking into those warm blue skies, military ter-ritory might be in plain sight, yet it is impossible to see.

I have always loved walking along Casuarina Beach at low tide — the great stretch of sand, one of the priceless attractions of old Darwin. It is a shifting landscape of oyster-crusted rocks, ribbed sand and currents slipping along hollows and rivulets, wet dogs barking their joy and harvesting driftwood and tennis balls from the claims of warm salt water, toddlers taking clumsy sand steps, stopping where they stumble to stare-down the mesmerising grits now crusting their palms. There is something reassuring about the long tidal ranges of Darwin, the slow silting up of the bays and harbours and the annual threat of cyclones. This primal insistence somehow holds Darwin's development ambitions, with their tilts against the lessons of natural history, in wondrous perspective.

Far away in the sky, a deceptively tiny plane, waving a feathering contrail of liquid droplets to those below, speeds from Asia to a city somewhere in the south-east of Australia. I think this is how the nation knows Darwin too, from a distance, in the abstract, as a canvas for projected ideas. The distance makes it all too easy to think of Darwin in terms of its craven local administrations, high living expenses, isolation, heavy drinking and pressing race relations. The city rewards deeper reflection. It brings into immediate focus questions that are transnational: climate change, resource management, migration, security and Australia's global future.

If Australian history properly starts in the north, then it seems the leading edge of its future is unfolding here too. Perhaps bearing the mantle of Charles Darwin is a proper responsibility for this place after all.

Acknowledgments

Preface

Note that Palmerston was the official name of the northern settlement until 1911, when the name Darwin was adopted. A satellite suburb to Darwin, also named Palmerston, was built in the 1980s to ease housing shortages. To avoid confusion, I use the name Darwin to cover all periods.

Suzanne Spunner's play *Dragged Screaming to Paradise* was published by Little Gem Publications, Darwin, in 1988.

I Building from the ruins

Bad Santa

Les Liddell's account of how Tennant Creek met the challenge of Cyclone Tracy's refugees is drawn from Liddell, L. (1994) Oral history interview by Francis Good, TS781, Northern Territory Archives Service, Darwin.

Dawn Lawrie is cited in Read, P. (1996) *Returning to Nothing: The Meaning of Lost Places*, Cambridge University Press, Cambridge, p. 154.

The report on survivors' psychological health is Chamberlain, E.R. (1981) *The Experience of Cyclone Tracy*, Department of Social Security, Australian Government Publishing Service, Canberra.

Australia's Pearl Harbor

The description of the Japanese bombings as 'the only significant battlefield of a modern mechanised war on Australian soil' is from De La Rue, C. (2005) 'The Battle of North Australia: The Archeology of a World War Two Airfield' in P. Bourke, S. Brockwell and C. Fredericksen (eds), *Darwin Archaeology: Aboriginal, Asian and European Heritage of Australia's Top End*, Charles Darwin University Press, Darwin, pp. 96–105.

Initial bombing figures were reported in 'The Darwin Air Raids: Full Scale Blitz, 15 Deaths Reported', *Townsville Daily Bulletin*, 21 February 1942, p. 5, while Prime Minister Curtin was cited in 'Darwin Heavily Bombed in 2 Raids, Attacks by 93 Planes: 4 Shot Down, Damage "Considerable"', *Argus*, 20 February 1942, p. 1.

Australia's 'Blue Water Strategy' is described in Rayner, R. (2002) *The Darwin Detachment: A Military and Social History*, Rudder Press, Wollongong, p. 13.

Information on what happened on the first day of the Japanese air raids is summarised at National Archives of Australia, *The Bombing of Darwin – Fact Sheet 195*, last viewed 29 Nov 2012 <www.naa.gov.au/collection/fact-sheets/fs195.aspx>.

'Capital of the second chance' is from Rothwell, N., 'Darwin: Capital of the Second Chance', *Weekend Australian Magazine*, 12 July 2003; reprinted in N. Rothwell (2007) *Another Country*, Black Inc., Melbourne.

Michael Taussig's description of heat is from Taussig, M. (2004) *My Cocaine Museum*, The University of Chicago Press, Chicago and London, p. 45.

Alexis Wright's thoughts on racial suppression are from an interview with Kerry O'Brien, 'Wright Wins Miles Franklin for Story of Homeland', *The 7.30 Report*, ABC TV, 21 June 2007, last viewed 20 August 2013 <www.abc.net.au/7.30/content/2007/s1958594.htm>.

A comprehensive account of Darwin's post-war

housing situation can be found in Dewar, M. (2010) *Darwin – No Place Like Home: Australia's Northern Capital in the 1950s through a Social History of Housing*, Historical Society of the Northern Territory, Darwin.

George Redmond's recollections of Darwin can be found in Redmond, G. (2001) *In the Eye of the Storm: Darwin's Development, Cyclone Tracy and Reconstruction*, Department of Transport and Works, Darwin.

The administrative compromise on housing plans is made by J. Wise, cited in Dewar (2010), *Darwin – No Place Like Home*, p. 129.

For information on Darwin's contemporary demography, see Charles Darwin University's The Northern Institute website at <www.cdu.edu.au/the-northern-institute/research-brief-series>. See also Carson, D. (2008) *Assessing the Population Impacts of Big Projects on Darwin: People Who Stayed Longer than Intended*, School for Social and Policy Research, Charles Darwin University, Darwin.

'A wide bay appearing'

Information on Charles Darwin is drawn from Browne, J. (2003) *Charles Darwin: Voyaging – Volume 1 of a Biography*, Pimlico, Random House, London (first ed. 1995). An account of the naming of Darwin Harbour can also be found in Lea, T. (2005) 'Introduction: The State of the North' in T. Lea and B. Wilson (eds), *The State of the North: Selected Papers from the 2003 Charles Darwin Symposia Series*, Charles Darwin University Press, Darwin, pp. xi–xvi; while the historian Alan Powell raises the issue of why the harbour wasn't 'discovered' by other explorers (for example, the Portuguese) in Powell, A. (2012) 'Charles Darwin, "Beagle", the Discovery and Naming of Port Darwin', *Journal of Northern Territory History* 23: pp. 77–93.

For a comprehensive account of Matthew Flinders's achievements, together with his edited diary records, see Flannery, T. (ed.) (2000) *Terra Australis: Matthew Flinders' Great Adventures in the Circumnavigation of Australia*, Text Publishing, Melbourne.

Citations from John Lort Stokes are from Stokes, J.L. (1846) *Discoveries in Australia; With an Account of the Coasts and Rivers Explored and Surveyed During the Voyage of H.M.S. Beagle, in the Years 1837–38–39–40–41–42–43. By Command of the Lords Commissioners of the Admiralty. Also a Narrative of Captain Owen Stanley's Visits to the Islands in the Arafura Sea*, Vol. 2, T. And W. Boone, London, e-book, last viewed 11 November 2012 <http://gutenberg.

net.au/ebooks/e00038.html>.

Stokes's obituary note about Charles Darwin for the *London Times* is cited in Holder, C.F. (1891) *Charles Darwin: His Life and Work*, Knickerbocker Press, New York, p. 21. Charles Darwin's lament about his seasickness and related loathing of the sea is drawn from Browne (2003), *Charles Darwin: Voyaging*, p. 178.

For information on how Aboriginal people managed the wetlands of Darwin, see Fredericksen, C., Brockwell, S. and Bourke, P. (2005) 'Introduction: Physical and Cultural Transformation in the Darwin Region' in P. Bourke, S. Brockwell and C. Fredericksen (eds), *Darwin Archaeology: Aboriginal, Asian and European Heritage of Australia's Top End*, Charles Darwin University Press, Darwin, p. 4.

Travelling distances and difficulties faced by early explorers and fortune seekers in the gold rush are given in De La Rue, K. (2004) *The Evolution of Darwin, 1869–1911*, Charles Darwin University Press, Darwin, p. 33.

Frank Alcorta summarises the South Australian ambition for an 'inexpensive penetration' of its northern colony in Alcorta, F. (1984) *Darwin Rebellion 1911–1919*, Northern Territory Government Printer, Darwin, p. x.

2 Dangerous proximities

Hooves and guns

Tony Roberts's account of pastoral brutalities can be found in Roberts, T., 'The Brutal Truth: What Happened in the Gulf Country', *The Monthly*, No. 51 (November 1999), last viewed 7 January 2013 <www.themonthly.com.au/issue/2009/november/1330478364/tony-roberts/brutal-truth>.

The way in which Aboriginal people describe the killing times is taken from Head, L. and Fullagar, R. (1997) 'Hunter–Gatherer Archaeology and Pastoral Contact: Perspectives from the Northwest Northern Territory, Australia', *World Archaeology (Special Issue: Culture Contact and Colonialism)*, 28(3): p. 419.

I have drawn my account of what happened to the sheep and other animals in the early pastoral experiments from Powell, A. (2009) *Far Country: A Short History of the Northern Territory*, Charles Darwin University Press, Darwin (first ed. 1982, MUP), pp. 75–77.

An account of the buffalo industry and how feral buffaloes have become a key part of the landscape is given in Robinson C. (2005) 'Buffalo

Hunting and the Feral Frontier of Australia's Northern Territory', *Social and Cultural Geography* 6(6): pp. 895–901.

Frank Alcorta provides information on the size of the Vestey and Bovril holdings in (1984) *Darwin Rebellion 1911–1919*, p. 22; see also Pearson, M. and Lennon, J. (2010) *Pastoral Australia: Fortunes, Failures and Hard Yakka – A Historical Overview 1788–1967*, CSIRO Publishing, Melbourne, p. 159. Nicolas Shaxson's account of the multinational cattle barons is enlightening: Shaxson, N. (2011) *Treasure Islands: Tax Havens and the Men Who Stole the World*, The Bodley Head, London, p. 35. A more concentrated account of beef industries in the north and the often poor management practices they suffered from is given in Kelly, J.H. (1971) *Beef in Northern Australia*, Australian National University Press, Canberra. Anthropologist Deborah Bird Rose reveals the terror of the pastoral runs, and the prowess of its drafted workers, in Rose, D.B. (1991) *Hidden Histories: Black Stories from Victoria River Downs, Humbert River and Wave Hill Stations*, Aboriginal Studies Press, Canberra.

For more detail on how the giant cattle companies blocked public infrastructure in the north, including railways, see Kelly, J.H. (1966) *Struggle for the North*, Australasian Book Society, Sydney, p. 3.

Casting for the Chauvels' film *Jedda* attracted much media interest. For one of many announcements about Hugh Wason Byers's role, see 'Cattleman to Act in Colour Film', *West Australian*, 17 June 1953, p. 13.

Humphrey McQueen revisited the politics behind the making of *Jedda* fifty years on from its debut at Darwin's Star Theatre on 3 January 1955: see McQueen, H., 'True Colours', *The Age*, 8 January 2005. Here McQueen describes Charles Chauvel's fascination with the hard men of the outback. Elsa Chauvel's account of dining with the 'sadist' Byers is in Chauvel, E. (1973) *My Life with Charles Chauvel*, Shakespeare Head Press, Sydney, pp. 134–35.

Byers's account of stopping didgeridoo songmen is narrated in Ogden, P. (1989) *Bradshaw via Coolibah: The History of Bradshaw's Run and Coolibah Station*, Historical Society of the Northern Territory, Darwin, pp. 39–40. A description of his face is given in Forrest, P., 'Wason's Bush Sweep', *NT News*, 27 October 1999, p. 28, describing Byers's win at the inaugural Tomaris Cup. He is also described in Schultz, C. and Lewis, D. (2008) *Beyond the Big*

Run: Station Life in Australia's Last Frontier, University of Queensland Press, St Lucia, pp. 170–75; and his cruelty is remembered by members of Pat Dodson's family in Kevin Keefe's (2002) *Paddy's Road: Life Stories of Patrick Dodson*, Aboriginal Studies Press, Canberra, pp. 134–35, 163–64.

Edgar Laytha's article on his time with the road builders making Australia's 'Burma Road' is in Laytha, E., 'Australia's Baby Singapore', *Saturday Evening Post*, 14 February 1942, 214(33), pp. 12–13, 48. Laytha's prophetic account of Japanese military strategy is in Laytha, E. (1937) *The March of Japan*, F.A. Stokes Co., New York.

For a report on the Byers case, see 'NT Cattleman Acquitted', *Sydney Morning Herald*, 7 October 1953, p. 4.

My account of the Mataranka cattle abuse case is drawn from NT Ombudsman (2010) *Report of Investigation into the Treatment of Cattle and Horses at Charles Darwin University Mataranka Station*, Vol. I, NT Ombudsman's Office, Darwin. <www.ombudsman.nt.gov.au/wp-content/uploads/2010/10/Investigation-into-the-Treatment-of-Cattle-Horses-at-CDU-Vol-I-Web-Friendly.pdf>.

The scholar Fiona Probyn-Rapsey describes

the hypocrisy of Australia's outcry over Indonesian slaughter practices in Probyn-Rapsey, F. (2013) 'Stunning Australia', *Humanimalia* 4(2): p. 88.

Flying darts

The Reverend Dunmore's eulogising account is cited in George Windsor Earl's account of the north's economic potential, in Earl G.W. (2002) *Enterprise in Tropical Australia*, Northern Territory University Press, Darwin, p. 4 (first ed. 1846). Earl had lived at Port Essington and was an influential expert on all things northern. T.H. Huxley's damning verdict is also from Earl (2002), *Enterprise in Tropical Australia*, p. 8.

Professor Bart Currie, an infectious disease specialist, having assessed the amount of drinking at Port Essington, is certain melioidosis was killing the men as much as malaria.

The description of Darwin's 'splendid isolation' is drawn from Powell, A. (2010) *Northern Voyagers: Australia's Monsoon Coast in Maritime History*, Australian Scholarly Publishing, Melbourne, p. 1.

The enlistment of mosquitoes to defend colonial acquisitions, using them as 'microbial swords', is outlined in McNeil, J.R. (2010) *Mosquito Empires:*

Ecology and War in the Greater Caribbean, 1620–1914, Cambridge University Press, Cambridge, p. 9. Using the vantage point of mosquitoes, the anthropologist Timothy Mitchell also describes how capitalism thrived in the space made available by the introduction of malaria in rural Egypt: see Mitchell, T. (2002) *Rule of Experts: Egypt, Techno-Politics, Modernity*, University of California Press, Berkeley.

Over the years Professor Peter Whelan has published widely on his research findings relating to mosquito control, the history of entomological work and key research findings from scientific studies. Indicative references include Russell R. and Whelan P. (1986) 'Seasonal Prevalence of Adult Mosquitoes at Casuarina and Leanyer, Darwin', *Australian Journal of Ecology* 11: pp. 99–105; Whelan, P. (1989) 'Integrated Mosquito Control in Darwin', *Arbovirus Research in Australia* 5: pp. 178–85; Jacups, S., Warchot, A. and Whelan, P. (2012) 'Anthropogenic Ecological Change and Impacts on Mosquito Breeding and Control Strategies in Salt-marshes, Northern Territory, Australia', *Eco-Health* 9(2): pp. 183–94. Professor Whelan generously arranged my access to the entomology library, including public health information and unpublished reports for committees of review and development inquiries. My account here draws on these readings and time spent with the entomologists, whom I consider the frontline soldiers of habitable Darwin.

Marilynne Paspaley's reminiscences about street fogging is cited from Paspaley, M. (2005) 'Finding the Spirit of Darwin', *Nineteenth Eric Johnson Memorial Lecture*, Northern Territory Arts and Museums, Darwin <http: //artsandmuseums. nt.gov.au/__data/assets/pdf_file/0007/114946/ occpaper58_ej19.pdf>.

Chromaphobia

For more on the Hakka–Punti conflict and its creation of refugee groups – the 'coolies' – see Cohen, M.L. (1968) 'The Hakka or "Guest People": Dialect as a Sociocultural Variable in Southeastern China', *Ethnohistory* 15(3): 237–92; Erbaugh, M. (1992) 'The Secret History of the Hakkas: The Chinese Revolution as a Hakka Enterprise', *The China Quarterly* 132: pp. 937–68; see also Giese, D. (1995) *Beyond Chinatown: Changing Perspectives on the Top End Chinese Experience*, National Library of Australia, Canberra, p. 43. On the Hakka in Darwin today, see Smith, R. (2012) *Hakka: The Diaspora Leading to the Northern Territory*, Hakka Association of the Northern Territory, Winnellie, NT.

Figures on the Chinese population in relation to Anglo settlers in February 1888 are from Alcorta (1984), *Darwin Rebellion*, p. xii; Yee, G. (2006) *Through Chinese Eyes: The Chinese Experience in the Northern Territory, 1874–2004*, Glenice Yee, Parap, p. 38.

Diane Giese's *Beyond Chinatown* (1995) describes the key architectural works made by Chinese labour. Robyn Smith has also done much to publicise Chinese contributions to the built environment: see Smith, R. (2008) 'Stone Houses: The Only Remnant of Darwin's Chinatown', *Historic Environment* 21(3): pp. 40–43.

Regina Ganter's provocation to understand Australian history from the north down is from Ganter, R. (2005) 'Turn the Map Upside Down', *Griffith Review* 9: p. 1, last viewed 27 November 2013 <https://griffithreview.com/edition-9-up-north/turning-the-map-upside-down>; see also Ganter, R. (2006) *Mixed Relations: Asian–Aboriginal Contact in North Australia*, University of Western Australia Publishing, Perth.

Information on the legal prejudices exacted

on the Chinese in Australia is from Jupp, J. (ed.) (2001) *The Australian People: An Encyclopedia of the Nation, Its People and Their Origins*, Cambridge University Press, Cambridge, p. 203. The impact of the White Australia Policy on the size of Darwin's Chinese population is drawn from Reynolds, H. (2003) *North of Capricorn: The Untold Story of Australia's North*, Allen & Unwin, Sydney, p. 107.

Elsie Masson was also the wife of anthropologist Bronislaw Malinowski. Her time working as an *au pair* for administrator Gilruth is described in Wayne, H. (1996) *The Story of a Marriage: The Letters of Bronislaw Malinowski and Elsie Masson — Vol. 1*, Routledge, London, p. xiv. Elsie Masson's description of Darwin is from Masson, E. (1915) *An Untamed Territory: The Northern Territory of Australia*, MacMillan, London, pp. 31–32.

The Commonwealth Inquiry into life in Darwin and the problem of white leisure is cited in Jones, T.G. (2005) *The Chinese in the Northern Territory* (3rd ed.), Charles Darwin University Press, Darwin, p. 114.

Susan Sickert's account of race relations in Broome is from Sickert, S. (2003) *Beyond the Lattice: Looking into Broome's Early Years*, Fremantle Press, Perth, p. 53.

Weddell's complaints can be found in Weddell, R.H. (1934) *Report on the Administration of the Northern Territory for the Year Ended 30th June, 1933*, Parliament of the Commonwealth of Australia, Canberra.

For Lily Ah Toy's story, see Ah Toy, L. (1979) Oral history interview by Ann McGrath, Northern Territory Archives Service, NTRS226, TSI, pp. 45, 48–49.

For Val McGinness story, see McGinness, V. (1979) Oral history interview by Janet Dickson, TS532, Northern Territory Archives, p. 7.

Information on Harry Chan is from Heatley, A. (1993) 'Chan, Harry (1918–1969)' in J. Ritchie and D. Langmore (eds), *Australian Dictionary of Biography, Vol. 13*, Australian National University, Canberra, last viewed 27 November 2013 <http://adb.anu.edu.au/biography/chan-harry-9722>.

Levelling the field

Information about the McGinness/McGuinness family was gathered from archival records, newspaper accounts, native title hearings and discussions with family descendents, especially Geoffrey (Jacko) Angeles. The account of the accident at Lucy Mine was reconstructed from an anonymous article, 'Accident at Lucy Claim', *Northern Territory Times and Gazette*, 30 November 1918, p. 11. It is also mentioned in the opening scenes of *Forced Legacy: The Story of Alyngdabu*, a play co-written by author, poet and playwright Kathy Mills with her daughter Ali Mills, about Kathy's grandmother, Alyngdabu, and her husband, Irishman Stephen McGuinness. *Forced Legacy* was additionally co-written and directed by Damian A. Pree and screened at Brown's Mart Theatre, 1–6 October 2013.

For information on what the 1967 Referendum did and did not achieve (it did not confer citizenship or voting rights, as is often claimed), see National Archives of Australia, *The 1967 Referendum – Fact Sheet 150*, last viewed 27 November 2013 <www.naa.gov.au/collection/fact-sheets/fs150.aspx>.

For information about Stephen McGinness's happy drinking character when in town, see 'For Auld Lang Syne', *Northern Territory Times*, 5 July 1927, p. 2. Stephen and Alyngdabu's granddaughter Kathy Mills describes the intentional politics behind Stephen's naming of the Lucy Tin Mine in the Native Title Tribunal hearing, *William Risk and Kathleen Mary Mills/McGinnis/Corporate*

Developments Pty Ltd/Northern Territory of Australia [2002] NNTTA 46, Brisbane, Application No. DO0I/77, Kathleen Mary Mills/McGinness affidavit, last viewed 23 September 2013 <www.nntt.gov.au/Future-Acts/Search-FA-Determinations/Documents/do0I_77_determination15042002.pdf>.

The newspaper account of the copper miners' deaths at Daly River is from 'The Daly River Proprietary Copper Mine', *Northern Territory Times and Gazette*, 20 June 1890, p. 3. The number of deaths and injuries exacted on Aboriginal people as part of the punitive raids sweeping across the Top End will never be known. On this, see discussion by Kathy De La Rue in *The Evolution of Darwin*, p. 80; Stephen Gray (2011) *The Protectors: A Journey through Whitefella Past*, Allen & Unwin, Sydney, pp. 31–32, and pp. 273–74, n. 6; and Elizabeth Povinelli (1993) *Labor's Lot: The Power, History and Culture of Aboriginal Action*, University of Chicago Press, Chicago, pp. 83, and pp. 282–83, nn. 37, 38. Corporal George Montague's evaluation report on the effectiveness of the Martini-Henry rifle for native retribution is cited in Harris, A. (2003) 'Hiding the Bodies: The Myth of the Humane Colonisation of Aboriginal Australia', *Aboriginal History* 27:

93; see also 'The Daly River Murders', *Northern Territory Times and Gazette*, 26 December 1885, pp. 2–3. For more on the power of the rifles and their ability to slay an elephant in its tracks, see Roberts (2009), 'The Brutal Truth'.

Joe McGinness's account of the poisoning of the Kungarakan people is in McGinness, J. (1991) *Son of Alyandabu: My Fight for Aboriginal Rights*, Queensland University Press, St Lucia, p. 8.

Harry Edwards, who married Margaret McGinniss, is briefly described in Stephen, M. (2009) *Contact Zones: Sport and Race in the Northern Territory, 1869–1953*, PhD Thesis, Charles Darwin University, p. 238, n. 6, last viewed 27 November 2013 <http://espace.cdu.edu.au/view/cdu:9206>.

Descriptions of the hunger children faced in Kahlin Compound and the fearful supervisors are from McGinness (1991) *Son of Alyandabu*, pp. 9, 10. Joe McGinness's later political exploits are well documented: see Reason in Revolt: Source Documents of Australian Radicalism, *McGinness, Joe (1914–2003)*, last viewed 24 September 2013 <www.reasoninrevolt.net.au/biogs/E000341b.htm>.

The author Xavier Herbert described Kahlin Compound in *Capricornia: A Novel* (1939) Angus &

Robertson, Sydney, p. 199. Herbert was temporarily a supervisor at Kahlin (1935–36), and came to know the McGinness family well, drawing on their history for his writings. Herbert collaborated with Val McGinness in an attempt to improve conditions for inmates. See also Stephen Gray's (2011) *The Protectors* for more on the men who rounded up Aboriginal people, and their rationales.

McGinness, V. (1984) Oral history interview with Janet Dickson, TS532, Northern Territory Archives, Tape 1, 12 and Tape 2, 9.

On the racial politics and history of sport in the Northern Territory, see Stephen, M. (2010) *Contact Zones: Sport and Race in the Northern Territory 1869–1953*, Charles Darwin University Press, Darwin.

Geoffrey (Jacko) Angeles published a prize-winning account of the health benefits of traditional fish trapping in the *Medical Journal of Australia*: Angeles, G.A. (2005) 'Fish Traps – A Significant Part of Our Health and Wellbeing', *Medical Journal of Australia*, 182: pp. 541–43. As Jacko promised, the magnificent story of 'Buffs' football is captured in Roberts, P. and Des Kootji, R. (1997) *Buffalo Legends*, Ronin Films, Australia.

3 Living it

Chromies, swampies and the kindness of strangers

'With over one in five non-Indigenous residents in Darwin admitting they had gone fishing at least once over the latest survey year' and other statistics on Darwin fishing can be found in West, L.D., Lyle, J.M., Matthews, S.R., Stark, K.E. and Steffe, A.S. (2012) *Survey of Recreational Fishing in the Northern Territory, 2009–10,* Fishery Report No. 109, Northern Territory Government, Australia, pp. 27, 31, 33.

The government pamphlet on fishing controls can be found at NT Fisheries, *Know Your Limits: Northern Territory Recreational Fishing Controls,* Northern Territory Government, Darwin, 2013, last viewed 27 November 2013 <www.nt.gov. au/d/Fisheries/rfc/limits/index.cfm>.

For a taste of the resentment over any threats to non-Indigenous fishing access, see Turner, E., 'Fishos Facing Fines', *NT News,* 17 May 2013, last viewed 17 June 2013 <dev.video.ntnews.com.au/ article/2013/05/17/321001_fishing.html>.

Aly de Groot explains her creative philosophy

and eco-critique in de Groot, A. *Underwater Basket Weaving*, 2013, last viewed 8 September 2013 <www.alydegroot.com.au/index.php/galleries/underwater-basket-weaving>; for more on the increasing 'seasickness' of our oceans and how critters like box jellyfish will flourish, even in the seas around Sydney, see Gershwin, L. (2013) *Stung! On Jellyfish Blooms and the Future of the Ocean*, University of Chicago Press, Chicago.

Heritage and rubble

For more on the Hotel Darwin and its 'distinctive canopy of blue Marseilles tiles', see Carment, D. (1996) *Looking at Darwin's Past: Material Evidence of European Settlement in Tropical Australia*, North Australia Research Unit, Australian National University, Darwin, p. 5. Kathy Stinson describes the National Trust's dramatic efforts to stop the demolition of the Hotel Darwin in Stinson, K. (2002) 'Historic Sites and Developmentalism: A Study of the Country Liberal Party's Policy on the Development of Darwin', *Journal of Northern Territory History* 13(17): pp. 15–23. The hotel's destruction and where the convention centre was eventually built is described in Dillon, M., 'A Decade of Dilemma over Convention Site', *Sunday Territorian* (Darwin), 19 June 2011, p. 31.

My account of the courtship of Heather Bell by Tom Harris and the early business of the Star Theatre is drawn from discussions with Tom Harris (junior) and analysis of Harris family memorabilia. Heather's refusal to pay the entrance fee for the Darwin baths is recounted in 'Darwin Police Court, Friday (Before Mr V. L. Lampe, S.M.)', *Northern Standard*, 19 June 1931, p. 5.

Humphrey McQueen gives details on the warnings given to the Chauvels about using Aboriginal actors in McQueen, H., 'True Colours', *The Age*, 8 January 2005.

Eating warm mangoes

Many of the observations in this chapter are drawn from interviews with locals, both recorded and informal, the viewing of creative works and my own experiences. The names of the young men and women have been changed, to preserve confidentiality. Tom Harris led me to Wayne Lennox Miles, who is an acute observer of Darwin's contradictions and beauties (as are others in the town's vibrant creative sector). Scholarly treatment of 'the Territorian' is given in Carment, D. (2007) *Territorianism: Politics and Identity in Australia's Northern Territory 1978–2001*, Australian Scholarly Publishing, Melbourne. Tony Clifton's revisiting of Darwin after many years absence can be found in Clifton, T., 'Lilypad of the Arafura', *The Monthly*, No. 8 (December 2005 – January 2006). It was only when I learnt that US military bases are named 'lilypads' when they are 'lighter' than a permanent garrison that I understood the irony of Tony's title (see 'Pin in the Map', Chapter 4).

4 Future Darwin

Rebellion to sameness

My account of Darwin's time as Australia's 'little Moscow' draws on Frank Alcorta (1984) *Darwin Rebellion* (see p. 101 for a description of the long march from the suburb of Parap to Government House, including the role of the effigy, and p. 104 for an account of Gilruth's rescue by military boat). Gilruth's battles with union protestors are also described in Powell, A. (1983) 'Gilruth, John Anderson (1871–1937)', Australian Dictionary of Biography, Australian National

University, Canberra, last viewed 19 July 2013 <http://adb.anu.edu.au/biography/gilruth-john-anderson-6393/text10927>. The Commonwealth Government did not renew Gilruth's appointment but convened a Royal Commission, headed by Justice Ewing, to inquire into Australia's third tilt against constitutional authority (joining the Rum Rebellion and the Eureka Stockade). His account of Gilruth as temperamentally unsuited for the appointment is in *Report on Northern Territory Administration*, pp. 5, 12, 16; Commonwealth Parliamentary Papers (1920–21), Vol. III, pp. 1653–69.

Key histories of Darwin's administration include Carment, D. (2005) *Australia's Northern Capital: A Short History of Darwin*, Historical Society of the Northern Territory, Darwin; Powell, A. (1988) *Far Country: A Short History of the Northern Territory*, Melbourne University Press, Carlton; De La Rue, K. (2004) *The Evolution of Darwin*, pp. 129–35; and, most recently, Clare Martin and Mickey Dewar's joint publication of interviews with successive Chief Ministers: Martin, C. and Dewar, M. (2012) *Speak for Yourself: Eight Chief Ministers Reflect on Northern Territory Self-Government*, Charles Darwin University Press, Darwin. My account also draws on interviews with Kon Vatskalis (ALP) and town planner Graham Bailey, and discussions with historian Robyn Smith, whose PhD dissertation focused on the record of the Country Liberal Party since self-government in 1978.

The struggles to realise a coordinated vision for Darwin in the pre- and post-war periods is given in Gibson, E. (1998) 'A Planner's Dream – A Citizen's Nightmare', *Australian Planner* 35(4): pp. 192–96. See also Gibson, E. (1997) *Bag-huts, Bombs and Bureaucrats: A History of the Impact of Town Planning and Compulsory Land Acquisition on the Town and People of Darwin 1937–1950*, Historical Society of the Northern Territory, Darwin. Gibson's account of McInnis's ill-fated critique of naval commandeering is on p. 194.

Darwin's 'Tracy trauma' house designs are briefly described in Carment (1996), *Looking at Darwin's Past*, p. 18; while Ken Todd gives a close account of the mismatch between post-cyclone reconstruction ambitions and the money made available in Todd, K. (2010) 'Darwin – Post-Tracy', *Royal Australian Planning Institute Journal* 17(3): pp. 192–96. The administrative conundrums of this period are usefully canvassed in George Redmond's (2001) *In the Eye of the Storm*.

Carceral city

Information on the Northern Territory's incarceration rates is from the Australian Bureau of Statistics (2013) *Corrective Services in Australia, September Quarter 2013*, Cat. 4512.0, p. 4; on violent sexual assaults, Australian Bureau of Statistics (2003) *Recorded Crimes – Victims, Australia, 2003*, Cat. 4510.0.

Professor Gelber's comments on the seismic defence policy shifts taking place under Australian noses are in Gelber, H. (2012) 'Australia's Geo-Political Strategy and the Defence Budget', *Quadrant*, LVI(6): 11. Information on Australia's shift to northern armament is drawn from Langtry, J.O. and Ball, D. (1991) *The Northern Territory in the Defence of Australia: Strategic and Operational Considerations*, ANU Press, Canberra, p. 82. Their comment on the time taken to respond after Cyclone Tracy is on p. 85.

The account of Captain Bradshaw's final wishes is drawn from 'Bradshaw Obituary', *Northern Territory Times*, 27 July 1916, p. 17.

Paul Toohey's account of US military sex crimes and their aftermath in local Australian communities is in Toohey, P., 'Oversexed and Over Here', *The Australian*, 27 October 2001, p. 23.

'Marines Come Ashore to Share Their Toys' is the headline for Byrne, C., *NT News*, 29 August 2013.

The accounts of defence force stress points after years of increasing demands funded by 'cuts' to non-essential items are drawn from Steward, C., 'Asylum Demands Breaking Navy Fleet', *The Australian*, 10 August 2012; Nicholson, B., 'Troops' Asylum Stress "as High as in Afghanistan"', *The Australian*, 3 December 2012; Rawlinson, C., 'Turn Back Boats Policy Doomed: Former ADF Chief', *ABC News*, 18 September 2013, last viewed 19 September 2013 <www.abc.net.au/news/2013-09-18/barrie-on-asylum-seeker-boat-policy-dound-to-fail/4965582>.

For more on the Defence Community Organisation and how it can support defence force families, see DCO, *What We Do*, Department of Defence, Australian Government, Canberra, 2013, last viewed 9 August 2013 <www.defence.gov.au/dco/What_we_do.htm>.

BaseWatch information on US military 'lily-pads' in Darwin can be found at BaseWatch, *US Military Base in Darwin*, 2013, last viewed 9 August 2013 <http://basewatch.org/>.

The two government-commissioned consultancy reports on the anticipated social impact of the US Marine Corps rotations list are NOETIC Solutions (2012) *Social Impact Assessment: United States Marine Corp Rotational Presence Phase 1 (Rotations of 200–250 US Marines into the Northern Territory)*, Report for the Department of Defence Force Posture Review Implementation Team, Australian Department of Defence, Canberra, and Deloitte Access Economics Pty Ltd (2013) *Social Impact Assessment of Potential Rotations of Up to 1,100 US Marines and Associated Equipment in Northern Australia*, Australian Department of Defence, Canberra.

Tollner, D., 'The Northern Territory Government Perspective', *Defending Australia: The US Military Presence in Northern Australia*, Charles Darwin University Seminar, 23 August 2013.

Journalist Alyssa Betts's account of the benefits of visiting military personnel for sex workers is at Betts, A., 'Seamen Ahoy – US Boys Meet NT Girls', *NT News*, 29 June 2010. Her discussion of the apparent tensions between different sex workers can be found in Betts, A., 'Sex Standoff over the Rub-and-Tug Racket', *NT News*, 9 September 2011.

Acknowledgments

I didn't know it consciously, but I have wanted to write this book for a long time, so my first thanks are due to Phillipa McGuinness, who gave me the opportunity to do it, and whose editorial team (the wondrous Uthpala Gunethilake and the sharp-eyed Tricia Dearborn) worked through the text with me so collaboratively. From there the list grows, as I met with serious generosity in multiple directions.

This book could not have been written without my many Darwin friends. These are the people who first told me about their lives or connected me to others, providing the impetus every researcher needs. Some have been acknowledged by name in this book; others cannot be acknowledged by name, in view of the sensitivity of their positions or of the material I was seeking. Some stories were given to me that are not in this book, for lack of space rather than interest. This includes the story of my brave, cheeky, swimming champion mother, Frances (Bobbie) Lea, whose extraordinary life tales I hope yet to properly tell.

I am indebted also to the many professionals who assisted my research requests, including the always helpful staff at the Northern Territory Library and the Northern Territory Archives;

and the office support and collegiality of folk at the Northern Institute at Charles Darwin University. Mr Yuri Shukost of the Department of Defence guided me through Defence procedures for accessing military personnel and other clearance requirements. This was done with the utmost professionalism, and while I realise the material canvassed here is confronting in parts, that I was free to write it is part of what Australia stands for and what the ADF defends. I am truly grateful for my thought-provoking interactions with honourable Defence Force members, past and present, and for the courtesy I was shown in accessing key people to talk to.

Professor Stephen Muecke not only encouraged the undertaking from the get-go, but endured walks and drafts, tolerating the ear- and the eye-pain of scattered ideas being hammered into shape. Even before I began, over morning toast in Oslo, Professor Marianne Lien told me I had to write such a book, convinced as she was that it would show an Australia others needed to know. Professor Ian Buchanan is another who has urged me to think about Darwin and its meanings for a long time. He too read drafts and fortified my sense of purpose. Professor Elizabeth Povinelli is a mentor, collaborator and friend. Thank you, Beth, for our crazy meals, walks and talks — may they long continue.

My colleagues in Gender and Cultural Studies and the wider School of Philosophical and Historical Inquiry at the University of Sydney not only provide an exceptional research community, but assisted with advice on everything from the eco-impact of catch-and-release fishing techniques (thank you Jodi Frawley) and suggested invigorating writing approaches. Fiona Probyn-Rapsey and the Human Animal Research Network provided reminders about the importance of the worlds that are usually excluded from social scientific writing, and gave permission to invoke these in a place, Darwin, which demands all its presences be acknowledged. Most valuable of all, Professor Barbara Caine kept close tabs on the project and provided a wider reading circle for first reactions.

Profound thanks also go to Emeritus Professor David Carment, the foremost historian of Northern Territory affairs, who met with me early and pointed me in important directions, posted material, made me more precise and never failed to be inspiring. David has been at the centre of a group of librarians, historians and political analysts who have created a growing body of material about northern history and political affairs that I was able to draw upon. Their work, done with little funding, is a public service that deserves wide recognition.

I thank the Australian Research Council for my present Queen Elizabeth II Research Fellowship, without which I would not have had the wherewithal to follow the trails this book provoked. My QEII Fellowship pursues two issues: 1) Can there be good policy in regional and remote Australia? and 2) What are some better ways to communicate any insights generated on this question? I have woven these twin concerns into this book, showing policy unfoldings and trying to bring these to life through words.

Finally, members of my family. My parents were informants and inspirations, both. Greg Moo, Elise Moo and Daniel Moo looked at material and talked to me bluntly about what was readable and what bored them silly. For the cups of tea, tolerance of sojourns, editorial guidance, love and support, I thank you. And for their insistent reminders that walks help words, I thank all our puppy dogs too.

Bibliography

'Accident at Lucy Claim', *Northern Territory Times and Gazette*,
30 November 1918.

Ah Toy, L. (1979) Oral history interview by Ann McGrath, Northern
Territory Archives Service, NTRS226, TSI.

Alcorta, F. (1984) *Darwin Rebellion 1911–1919*, Northern Territory
Government Printer, Darwin.

Angeles, G.A. (2005) 'Fish Traps – A Significant Part of Our Health and
Wellbeing', *Medical Journal of Australia* 182: 541–43.

Australian Bureau of Statistics (2003) *Recorded Crimes – Victims, Australia,
2003*, Cat. 4510.0.

Australian Bureau of Statistics (2013) *Corrective Services in Australia*,
September Quarter 2013, Cat. 4512.0.

BaseWatch 2013, *US Military Base in Darwin*, BaseWatch, Darwin <http://
basewatch.org/>.

Betts, A., 'Seamen Ahoy – US Boys Meet NT Girls', *NT News*,
29 June 2010.

——, 'Sex Standoff over the Rub-and-Tug Racket', *NT News*,
9 September 2011.

Bourke, P., Brockwell, S. and Fredericksen, C. (eds) (2005) *Darwin
Archaeology: Aboriginal, Asian and European Heritage of Australia's Top End*,
Charles Darwin University Press, Darwin.

Bradshaw Obituary, *Northern Territory Times*, 27 July 1916.

Browne, J. (2003) *Charles Darwin: Voyaging – Volume 1 of a Bibliography*,
Pimlico, Random House, London (first ed. 1995).

Byrne, C., 'Marines Come Ashore to Share Their Toys', *NT News*, 29
August 2013.

Carment, D. (1996) *Looking at Darwin's Past: Material Evidence of European
Settlement in Tropical Australia*, North Australia Research Unit,

Australian National University, Darwin.

—— (2005) *Australia's Northern Capital: A Short History of Darwin*, Historical Society of the Northern Territory, Darwin.

—— (2007) *Territorianism: Politics and Identity in Australia's Northern Territory 1978–2001*, Australian Scholarly Publishing, Melbourne.

Carson, D. (2008) *Assessing the Population Impacts of Big Projects on Darwin: People Who Stayed Longer than Intended*, School for Social and Policy Research, Charles Darwin University, Darwin.

'Cattleman to Act in Colour Film', *West Australian*, 17 June 1953.

Chamberlain, E.R. (1981) *The Experience of Cyclone Tracy*, Department of Social Security, Australian Government Publishing Service, Canberra.

Chauvel, E. (1973) *My Life With Charles Chauvel*, Shakespeare Head Press, Sydney.

Clifton, T. (2005) 'Lilypad of the Arafura', *The Monthly*, No. 8 (December 2005 – January 2006).

Cohen, M.L. (1968) 'The Hakka or "Guest People": Dialect as a Sociocultural Variable in Southeastern China', *Ethnohistory* 15(3): 237–92.

'The Daly River Murders', *Northern Territory Times and Gazette*, 26 December 1885.

'The Daly River Proprietary Copper Mine', *Northern Territory Times and Gazette*, 20 June 1890.

'The Darwin Air Raids: Full Scale Blitz, 15 Deaths Reported', *Townsville Daily Bulletin*, 21 February 1942.

'Darwin Heavily Bombed in 2 Raids, Attacks by 93 Planes: 4 Shot Down, Damage "Considerable"', *Argus*, 20 February 1942.

'Darwin Police Court, Friday (Before Mr V. L. Lampe, S.M.)', *Northern Standard*, 19 June 1931.

Gershwin, L. (2013) *Stung! On Jellyfish Blooms and the Future of the Ocean*, University of Chicago Press, Chicago.

de Groot, A. (2013) *Underwater Basket Weaving* <www.alydegroot.com.au/index.php/galleries/underwater-basket-weaving>.

Defence Community Organisation, *What We Do*, Department of Defence, Australian Government, Canberra, 2013 <www.defence.gov.au/dco/What_we_do.htm>.

De La Rue, K. (2004) *The Evolution of Darwin, 1869–1911*, Charles Darwin University Press, Darwin.

Deloitte Access Economics Pty Ltd (2013) *Social Impact Assessment of*

Bibliography

Potential Rotations of Up to 1,100 US Marines and Associated Equipment in Northern Australia, Australian Department of Defence, Canberra.

Dewar, M. (2010) *Darwin: No Place Like Home – Australia's Northern Capital in the 1950s through a Social History of Housing*, Historical Society of the Northern Territory, Darwin.

Dillon, M., 'A Decade of Dilemma over Convention Site', *Sunday Territorian* (Darwin) 19 June 2011.

Earl G.W. (2002) *Enterprise in Tropical Australia*, Northern Territory University Press, Darwin (first ed. 1846).

Erbaugh, M. (1992) 'The Secret History of the Hakkas: The Chinese Revolution as a Hakka Enterprise', *China Quarterly* 132: 937–68.

Flannery, T. (ed) (2000) *Terra Australis: Matthew Flinders' Great Adventures in the Circumnavigation of Australia*, Text Publishing, Melbourne.

'For Auld Lang Syne', *Northern Territory Times*, 5 July 1927.

Forrest, P., 'Wason's Bush Sweep', *NT News*, 27 October 1999.

Ganter, R. (2005) 'Turn the Map Upside Down', *Griffith Review*, No. 9 <https://griffithreview.com/edition-9-up-north/turning-the-map-upside-down>.

—— (2006) *Mixed Relations: Asian Aboriginal Contact in North Australia*, University of Western Australia Publishing, Perth.

Gelber, H. (2012) 'Australia's Geo-Political Strategy and the Defence Budget', *Quadrant* LVI(6): 11–9.

Gibson, E. (1997) *Bag-huts, Bombs and Bureaucrats: A History of the Impact of Town Planning and Compulsory Land Acquisition on the Town and People of Darwin 1937–1950*, Historical Society of the Northern Territory, Darwin.

—— (1998) 'A Planner's Dream – A Citizen's Nightmare', *Australian Planner* 35(4): 192–96.

Giese, D. (1995) *Beyond Chinatown: Changing Perspectives on the Top End Chinese Experience*, National Library of Australia, Canberra.

Gray, S. (2011) *The Protectors: A Journey Through Whitefella Past*, Allen & Unwin, Sydney.

Harris, A. (2003) 'Hiding the Bodies: The Myth of the Humane Colonisation of Aboriginal Australia', *Aboriginal History* 27: 79–104.

Head, L. and Fullagar, R. (1997) 'Hunter–Gatherer Archaeology and Pastoral Contact: Perspectives from the Northwest Northern Territory, Australia', *World Archaeology (Special Issue: Culture Contact and Colonialism)* 28(3): 418–28.

Herbert, X. (1939) *Capricornia: A Novel*, Angus & Robertson, Sydney.

Holder, C.F. (1891) *Charles Darwin: His Life and Work*, Knickerbocker Press, New York.

Jacups, S., Warchot, A. and Whelan P. (2012) 'Anthropogenic Ecological Change and Impacts on Mosquito Breeding and Control Strategies in Salt-marshes, Northern Territory, Australia', *EcoHealth* 9(2): 183–94.

Jones, T.G. (2005) *The Chinese in the Northern Territory* (3rd ed.), Charles Darwin University Press, Darwin.

Jupp, J. (ed.) (2001) *The Australian People: An Encyclopedia of the Nation, Its People and Their Origins*, Cambridge University Press, Cambridge.

Keefe, K. (2002) *Paddy's Road: Life Stories of Patrick Dodson*, Aboriginal Studies Press, Canberra.

Kelly, J.H. (1966) *Struggle for the North*, Australasian Book Society, Sydney.

—— (1971) *Beef in Northern Australia*, Australian National University Press, Canberra.

Langtry, J.O. and Ball, D. (1991) *The Northern Territory in the Defence of Australia: Strategic and Operational Considerations*, ANU Press, Canberra.

Laytha, E. (1937) *The March of Japan*, F.A. Stokes C., New York.

——, 'Australia's Baby Singapore', *Saturday Evening Post*, 14 February 1942, 214(33): 12–3.

Lea, T. and Wilson, B. (eds) (2005) *The State of the North: Selected Papers from the 2003 Charles Darwin Symposia Series*, Charles Darwin University Press, Darwin.

Liddell, L. (1994) Oral history interview by Francis Good, TS781, Northern Territory Archives Service, Darwin.

McGinness, J. (1991) *Son of Alyandabu: My Fight for Aboriginal Rights*, Queensland University Press, St Lucia.

McGinness, V. (1984) Oral history interview with Janet Dickson, TS532, Northern Territory Archives.

McNeil, J.R. (2010) *Mosquito Empires: Ecology and War in the Greater Caribbean, 1620–1914*, Cambridge University Press, Cambridge.

McQueen, H., 'True Colours', *The Age*, 8 January 2005.

Martin, C. and Dewar, M. (2012) *Speak for Yourself: Eight Chief Ministers Reflect on Northern Territory Self-Government*, Charles Darwin University Press, Darwin.

Masson, E. (1915) *An Untamed Territory: The Northern Territory of Australia*, Macmillan, London.

Bibliography

Mills, K. with Mills, A., *Forced Legacy: The Story of Alyngdabu* (play). Additionally co-written for performance by Damian A. Pree.

Mitchell, T. (2002) *Rule of Experts: Egypt, Techno-Politics, Modernity*, University of California Press, Berkeley.

National Archives of Australia, *The 1967 Referendum – Fact Sheet 150*, Australian Government, Canberra, 2013 <www.naa.gov.au/ collection/fact-sheets/fs150.aspx>.

National Archives of Australia, *The Bombing of Darwin – Fact Sheet 195*, Australian Government, Canberra, 2013 <www.naa.gov.au/ collection/fact-sheets/fs195.aspx>.

Native Title Tribunal Hearing, *William Risk and Kathleen Mary Mills/ McGinnis/Corporate Developments Pty Ltd/Northern Territory of Australia* [2002] NNTTA 46, Brisbane, Application No. DO01/77, Kathleen Mary Mills/McGinness affidavit <www.nntt.gov.au/ Future-Acts/Search-FA-Determinations/Documents/do01_77_ determination15042002.pdf>.

Nicholson, B., 'Troops' Asylum Stress "as High as in Afghanistan"', *The Australian*, 3 December 2012.

NOETIC Solutions (2012) *Social Impact Assessment: United States Marine Corp Rotational Presence Phase 1 (Rotations of 200–250 US Marines into the Northern Territory)*, Report for the Department of Defence Force Posture Review Implementation Team, Australian Department of Defence, Canberra.

'NT Cattleman Acquitted', *Sydney Morning Herald*, 7 October 1953.

NT Fisheries, *Know Your Limits: Northern Territory Recreational Fishing Controls*, Northern Territory Government, Darwin, 2013 <www.nt.gov.au/d/ Content/File/p/Fish_Rep/Recreational_Fishing_Controls.pdf>.

Ogden, P. (1989) *Bradshaw via Coolibah: The History of Bradshaw's Run and Coolibah Station*, Historical Society of the Northern Territory, Darwin.

Ombudsman NT, *Report of Investigation into the Treatment of Cattle and Horses at Charles Darwin University Mataranka Station*, Vol. 1, NT Ombudsman's Office, Darwin, 2010 <www.ombudsman.nt.gov.au/wp-content/ uploads/2010/10/Investigation-into-the-Treatment-of-Cattle-Horses-at-CDU-Vol-1-Web-Friendly.pdf>.

Paspaley, M., *Finding the Spirit of Darwin*, Nineteenth Eric Johnson Memorial Lecture, Northern Territory Arts and Museums, Darwin, 2005 <http://artsandmuseums.nt.gov.au/__data/assets/pdf_ file/0007/114946/occpaper58_ej19.pdf>.

Pearson, M. and Lennon, J. (2010) *Pastoral Australia: Fortunes, Failures and Hard Yakka – A Historical Overview 1788–1967*, Melbourne, CSIRO Publishing.

Povinelli, E. (1993) *Labor's Lot: The Power, History and Culture of Aboriginal Action*, The University of Chicago Press, Chicago.

Powell, A. (1983) 'Gilruth, John Anderson (1871–1937)', *Australian Dictionary of Biography* <http://adb.anu.edu.au/biography/gilruth-john-anderson-6393/text10927>.

—— (2009) *Far Country: A Short History of the Northern Territory*, Charles Darwin University Press, Darwin (first ed. 1982, MUP).

—— (2010) *Northern Voyagers: Australia's Monsoon Coast in Maritime History*, Australian Scholarly Publishing, Melbourne.

—— (2012) 'Charles Darwin, "Beagle", the Discovery and Naming of Port Darwin', *Journal of Northern Territory History* 23: 77–93.

Probyn-Rapsey, F. (2013) 'Stunning Australia', *Humanimalia* 4(2): 84–100.

Rawlinson, C., 'Turn Back Boats Policy Doomed: Former ADF chief', *ABC News*, 18 September 2013 <www.abc.net.au/news/2013-09-18/barrie-on-asylum-seeker-boat-policy-dound-to-fail/4965582>.

Rayner, R. (2002) *The Darwin Detachment: A Military and Social History*, Rudder Press, Wollongong.

Read, P. (1996) *Returning to Nothing: The Meaning of Lost Places*, Cambridge University Press, Cambridge.

Reason in Revolt (2005) *McGinness, Joe (1914–2003)* <www.reasoninrevolt.net.au/biogs/E000341b.htm>.

Redmond, G. (2001) *In the Eye of the Storm: Darwin's Development, Cyclone Tracy and Reconstruction*, Department of Transport and Works, Darwin.

Report on Northern Territory Administration, *Commonwealth Parliamentary Papers* (1920–21), Vol. III.

Reynolds, H. (2003) *North of Capricorn: The Untold Story of Australia's North*, Allen & Unwin, Sydney.

Ritchie, J. and Langmore, D. (eds) (1993) *Australian Dictionary of Biography, Vol. 13*, Australian National University, Canberra.

Roberts, P. and Des Kootji, R. (1997) *Buffalo Legends*, Ronin Films, Australia.

Roberts, T. (1999) 'The Brutal Truth: What Happened in the Gulf Country' *The Monthly*. No. 51 (November 1999) <www.themonthly.com.au/issue/2009/november/1330478364/tony-roberts/brutal-

truth>.

Robinson C. (2005) 'Buffalo Hunting and the Feral Frontier of Australia's Northern Territory', *Social and Cultural Geography* 6(6): 895–901.

Rose, D.B. (1991) *Hidden Histories: Black Stories from Victoria River Downs, Humbert River and Wave Hill Stations*, Aboriginal Studies Press, Canberra.

Rothwell, N., 'Darwin: Capital of the Second Chance', *Weekend Australian Magazine*, 12 July 2003.

—— (2007) *Another Country*, Black Inc., Melbourne.

Russell, R. and Whelan, P. (1986) 'Seasonal Prevalence of Adult Mosquitoes at Casuarina and Leanyer, Darwin', *Australian Journal of Ecology* 11: 99–105.

Schultz, C. and Lewis, D. (2008) *Beyond the Big Run: Station Life in Australia's Last Frontier*, University of Queensland Press, St Lucia.

Shaxson, N. (2011) *Treasure Islands: Tax Havens and the Men Who Stole the World*, The Bodley Head, London.

Smith, R. (2008) 'Stone Houses: The Only Remnant of Darwin's Chinatown', *Historic Environment* 21(3): 40–43.

Sickert, S. (2003) *Beyond the Lattice: Looking into Broome's Early Years*, Fremantle Press, Perth.

Smith, R. (2012) *Hakka: The Diaspora Leading to the Northern Territory*, Hakka Association of the Northern Territory, Winnellie, NT.

Spunner, S. (1988) *Dragged Screaming to Paradise*, Little Gem Publications, Darwin.

Stephen, M. (2009) *Contact Zones: Sport and Race in The Northern Territory, 1869–1953*, PhD Thesis, Charles Darwin University, available at <http://espace.cdu.edu.au/view/cdu:9206>.

—— (2010) *Contact Zones: Sport and Race in the Northern Territory 1869–1953*, Charles Darwin University Press, Darwin.

Steward, C., 'Asylum Demands Breaking Navy Fleet', *The Australian*, 10 August 2012.

Stinson, K. (2002) 'Historic Sites and Developmentalism: A Study of the Country Liberal Party's Policy on the Development of Darwin', *Journal of Northern Territory History* 13(17): 15–23.

Stokes, J.L. (1846) *Discoveries in Australia; With an Account of the Coasts and Rivers Explored and Surveyed During the Voyage of H.M.S. Beagle, in the Years 1037–38–39–40–41–42–43. By Command of the Lords Commissioners of the Admiralty. Also a Narrative of Captain Owen Stanley's Visits to the Islands in the Arafura Sea*, Vol. 2, T. And W. Boone, London, e-book <http://gutenberg.net.au/ebooks/e00038.html>.

Taussig, M. (2004) *My Cocaine Museum*, University of Chicago Press, Chicago.

Todd, K. (2010) 'Darwin – Post-Tracy', *Royal Australian Planning Institute Journal*, 17(3): 192–96.

Tollner, D., 'The Northern Territory Government Perspective', *Defending Australia: The US Military Presence in Northern Australia*, Charles Darwin University Seminar, 23 August 2013.

Toohey, P., 'Oversexed and Over Here', *The Australian*, 27 October 2001.

Turner, E., 'Fishos Facing fines', *NT News*, 17 May 2013 <dev.video.ntnews.com.au/article/2013/05/17/321001_fishing.html>.

Wayne, H. (1996) *The Story of a Marriage: The Letters of Bronislaw Malinowski and Elsie Masson – Vol. 1*, Routledge, London.

Weddell, R.H. (1934) *Report on the Administration of the Northern Territory for the Year Ended 30th June, 1933*, Parliament of the Commonwealth of Australia, Canberra.

West, L.D., Lyle, J.M., Matthews, S.R., Stark, K.E. and Steffe, A.S. (2012) *Survey of Recreational Fishing in the Northern Territory, 2009–10*, Fishery Report No. 109, Northern Territory Government, Australia.

Whelan, P.I. (1989) 'Integrated Mosquito Control in Darwin', *Arbovirus Research in Australia* 5: 178–185.

'Wright Wins Miles Franklin for Story of Homeland', *The 7.30 Report*, ABC, interview with Alexis Wright by Kerry O'Brien, 21 June 2007 <www.abc.net.au/7.30/content/2007/s1958594.htm>.

Yee, G. (2006) *Through Chinese Eyes: The Chinese Experience in the Northern Territory, 1874–2004*, Glenice Yee, Parap.

CASUARINA
BEACH

LEANYER
SWAMP

RAPID
CREEK

DARWIN
INTERNATIONAL
AIRPORT

EAST
POINT

FANNIE
BAY

MINDIL
BEACH

MYILLY BEACH
HERITAGE
PRECINCT

DARWIN

ESPLANADE

CBD

PORT
DARWIN

EAS
ARM